Where I Come From

Where I Come From

As Told To
Bryan Woolley

Number Two: A. C. Greene Series

University of North Texas Press
Denton, Texas

The paper in this book meets the minimum
requirements of the American National Standard
for Permanence of Paper for Printed Library
Materials, Z39.48.1984

Permissions
University of North Texas Press
PO Box 311336
Denton, TX 76203-1336
940-565-2142

Library of Congress Cataloging-in-Publication Data

Where I come from as told to Bryan Woolley.
    p. cm. — (A.C. Greene series ; no. 2)
ISBN 1-57441-164-0 (cloth : alk. paper)
1. Texas—Biography. I. Woolley, Bryan. II. Series
CT262 .W44 2003
920.0764'5—dc21

                                2003005223

Number Two: A. C. Greene Series

Unless otherwise noted, all photographs
are used courtesy of *The Dallas Morning News*.
Design by Angela Schmitt

For Lisa Kresl

Thanks for everything

Contents

Introduction   *1*

Kenneth Irby, orphan   *5*

Tony Zoppi, friend of stars   *11*

Jennifer Nguyen, war exile   *17*

Lois Adair, saloonkeeper   *23*

Clebo Rainey, performance poet   *29*

Jeanette Crumpler, the Tomato Lady   *35*

Frank Rush, pioneer entertainer   *41*

Denise Brown, member of the French Resistance   *47*

Burt Finger, gallery owner   *57*

Kenneth Adams, shoeshine man   *63*

James Jennings, back-roads traveler   *67*

Ed Seay Sr., model builder   *73*

Oksana Marchenko, new citizen   *81*

Beatrice Woolley, mother   *87*

Dale Long, bomb survivor   *95*

Terry Baker, finder of lost heroes   *101*

Gwendolyn Leakey, singer and yodeler   *107*

Frances James, the Cemetery Lady   *113*

Aki, hair stylist and potter   *119*

Etta Maberry, doing whatever had to be done   *125*

Lindon Dodge, paraplegic   *131*

R. L. Griffin, blues singer   *135*

Herbert Shore, gerontologist   *141*

Leo Laufer, Holocaust survivor   *147*

James Bell, firefighter   *165*

Ann Cushing Gantz, painter   *171*

John Hardman, puppeteer   *177*

Abel Reyna, history teacher   *185*

Sam Baker, public radio host   *191*

Big Bill Johnson, the Singing Drywall Man   *197*

Alfred Martinez, restaurateur   *203*

Pat Arnold, dog lover   *209*

Bob Walker, barbecue chef   *215*

Billy Roy Switzer, one-man band   *221*

Paul Hastings, singing store greeter   *227*

Quida Johnson, schoolteacher   *233*

Bob Colombe, Lakota barber   *239*

Frank Joseph, rabbi disk jockey   *245*

Efren Ortega, priest   *251*

Netha Stanton, actress   *257*

Fred Bruner, defense attorney   *263*

Al Cornelius, county judge   *269*

Artist Thornton, helper of young people   *275*

INTRODUCTION

During my long career as a journalist, I've learned that everybody has stories to tell and, given a willing listener, they're happy to tell them. In former times, they would have had plenty of listeners. Families sat together on front porches on summer nights or around stoves during winter evenings and told of things that happened to them or to their parents or to more distant ancestors. In this way, a family's history and folklore were passed down through the generations.

Nowadays, people don't sit together and swap stories. The stories most of us receive now were made in Hollywood and come to us via movie and television screens. As a result, many Americans born during the past fifty years have almost no knowledge of their own family histories. They've lost their roots. They have little or no idea where they came from.

In 1999, Lisa Kresl, the assistant managing editor in charge of the feature sections of *The Dallas Morning News*, had an idea: Take a tape recorder into the communities of North Texas and ask "ordinary" people—people who aren't rich or famous or powerful and are never in the news—to tell about their lives, especially their past, and how they became whom they became.

The tapes would be edited, of course, because such conversations always contain digressions, interruptions, memory lapses, and backtrackings. But the stories would be told in the tellers' own words, unmediated by the reporter's voice. They would be published as a regular feature in the *Morning News*, and the feature would be called "Where I Come From."

For me, "Where I Come From" was a dream assignment. I had grown up in an isolated West Texas mountain town that few radio waves and no television waves could reach. I spent many childhood hours on the long screened porch of our house, listening to my grandmother and her brothers and sisters and in-laws talk about people they had known and things that had happened as far back as the 1890s, when they were children. They told even older stories that they had heard from their parents.

Those hours on the porch were the beginning of my passion for history, and especially for folk history. Folk history and folk auto-biography—the kind of narrative written down by old cowboys and Texas Rangers and pioneer wives and printed in self-pub-lished books, and the kind gathered from old-timers by small-town newspaper reporters for their local weeklies—these always have been dear to me. They lack academic sophistication and, some-times, historical accuracy, but they have plenty of juice and flavor. And they often become sources for the academic historians who come along after the narrators are dead.

At first, "Where I Come From" was a weekly feature that ran every Sunday. But finding the people to interview, conducting the interviews and transcribing and editing the narratives turned out to be more time-consuming than Lisa and I had expected. "Where I Come From" was taking me away for too long from my other reporting and writing duties. So we began running it on a biweekly basis.

Judging from the volume of letters and phone calls, many read-ers loved "Where I Come From." In an italic paragraph at the end of each story, we invited readers to suggest someone they knew who might be good subject for the feature. In this way, people whom I never would have found on my own got their stories told.

The feature ran from May 16, 1999, to December 17, 2000. Forty-nine people narrated their stories to me. Among them were an orphan boy who lived in a movie theater; a refugee who traveled a long road to Texas after the fall of Saigon; a ballet teacher who as a teenager joined the French Resistance against the Nazis; a rabbi who was also a country-music disc jockey; a man who survived Auschwitz; a woman who spends her life saving abandoned dogs; a South Dallas blues singer; a one-man band from Denton; a professional barbecue cook who was hanging up his apron and retiring, and a shoeshine man who's also a minister. Forty-three of the "Where I Come From" narratives are included in this book. I've not tried to update them. The stories are presented here just as I first heard them. I enjoyed listening to every one of them. I treasure the warmth, the empathy and the laughter that often happened between their narrators and me.

It's a pleasure to pass along these stories to new readers, and to offer them a new life outside the ephemeral pages of the newspaper. I thank *The Dallas Morning News* for giving me permission to reprint them and the portraits that accompanied them. I also thank the photographers of the *News*, whose work has accompanied and enhanced many, many stories of mine, and Hector Cantu, who edited the pieces and caught my errors, and, especially, Lisa Kresl, whose idea it all was. And I thank Ronald Chrisman of the University of North Texas Press for his help in making these stories into a book.

Kenneth Irby in the usher's dressing room at the Majestic Theater, where he once lived secretly as a homeless teenage orphan in the early '60s. Courtesy *The Dallas Morning News*, Irwin Thompson, photographer.

Kenneth Irby

*Kenneth and Lovita Irby married when they were
teenagers working at two of the big movie
theaters that used to line Elm Street in Dallas.
They now own the Bluebonnet Art Gallery in
DeSoto, Texas. This is Kenneth's story.*

My mother married when she was thirteen. My father was eighteen at the time. I was born in Dallas at Florence Nightingale Hospital in 1947. I came first, and nine or ten or eleven months later, there would be another boy. There were six boys in my family.

My father was a truck driver. Little did I know when I was young that he was an alcoholic, but he was. We knew that he drank, and that just became part of our life as his kids. When I was ten years old, I had to go around and hunt my dad every Friday night. If I found him before he spent his whole paycheck, we had a good week. If I didn't find him till Sunday, then we suffered the whole week.

Consequently, we moved around Dallas a lot, because back then, if you didn't pay the rent, you had to get out. There aren't many elementary schools I didn't go to, because we moved so much.

Having five brothers and me being the oldest, I felt responsible for them. My mother was a very kind lady, but she was weak with my father. She always let him do pretty much what he wanted to do, and drinking was his main goal, it seemed.

When I was thirteen, I moved in with my grandmother and grandfather. I had an uncle, Art Cooley, who was just six months older than me, and we ran around East Dallas together. When I was fifteen and Art had turned sixteen, he was working at the Majestic Theater, and he got me an interview with Bob White, the manager. Bob said, "Sure. If you're kin to Art Cooley, you've got a job here."

It was like hitting the lights of Broadway all of a sudden. I was an usher at the Majestic Theater! I was making seventy-five cents an hour! That was in 1963.

Before my time, there were more theaters on Elm Street than even in Hollywood. The Majestic, the Capitol, the Melba, the Old Mill, the Palace, the Tower, the Capri. Elm Street was the showplace of the whole world. When I worked there, only the Majestic, the Tower, the Palace and the Capri remained.

Interstate Theaters owned them all except the Capri. Interstate had theaters from Dallas to Chicago. They had theaters in California and every little town in Texas. Hundreds of theaters.

The Majestic was the most glamorous of them all. A lot of movies premiered at the Majestic because Dallas was the headquarters of Interstate. *The Great Escape* premiered at the Majestic. Steve McQueen and all the stars came. John Wayne premiered *Hatari* there. He came to Dallas a lot. Those premieres were a big deal. More than 800 people would show up.

We got all the first-run shows, and the suburban theaters didn't get them till many months later. So people came downtown to the movies. Everybody dressed up. Nice dresses, suits. And the crowds were just huge.

Everything was very formal at the Majestic. The ticket-taker wore a tuxedo every day. The ushers wore nice double-breasted uniforms. We were given instructions on the proper way to do things, from the way you stood on your aisle to how to fill a mustard bottle. Everything was geared to the customer's comfort and pleasure. It was an honor to work there.

When I was sixteen, my mother passed away. She was thirty-two. She had a cerebral hemorrhage. They called me at the theater and told me my mom was at Parkland and she had passed away. All of a sudden, there was five brothers who had no home. I had to make sure they were taken care of.

Two went to live with my mother's sister. One got adopted by a cousin. One went to live with our father's mother in Tyler. The brother next to me, Glenn, was fifteen. He was old enough to go off on his own. He later became a CPA.

When Mom died, she had nothing. I had to pay for her funeral. I went to Dudley M. Hughes Funeral Home over on Jefferson, and Dudley was a nice man. He said, "Well, what do you have in collateral?" I said, "Nothing. The shirt off my back." He said, "Well, how much can you pay me?" I said, "What I'm making at the theater, I could probably pay you $10 a month." He said, "That's fine." So we had a real nice funeral for my mother. I paid $10 a month for years.

A few months after that, my grandmother passed away. So I found myself homeless. I went to Mr. White and asked him, "Hey, do you mind if I live in the ushers' dressing room for a while?" Mr. White said he didn't care. I lived down there about six months. Nobody knew it.

I was going to Crozier Technical High School, which was just down the street. I would walk to school and walk back to work every day. It was very convenient.

After about six months, the mother of another usher, Doug Brown, heard I was living in the theater. She told Doug to bring me home, that I could live with them. They lived in a little house behind a dentist's office. Their job was to clean the dentist's office, and the dentist let them live in the house. I lived with them about six months, then went and lived with my aunt for about six months, and then Lovita and I got married.

Lovita Choat was an usherette at the Tower Theater. We were both eighteen. After we got married, two of my brothers lived with us.

Lovita had a mother and father. They owned a frame shop and lived in Kessler Park. She was one of the few kids who worked at the theaters who had parents.

Mostly we were a bunch of dysfunctional kids who came together and formed a great friendship. Most of us didn't have mothers or fathers, or at least mothers or fathers who cared. Everybody was pretty much in the same boat. So the kids who worked at the theaters just became our own family. We still get together for a reunion every year.

I dropped out of school at Crozier because I thought the theater was going to be my career for the rest of my life. Mr. White put me in a management trainee program. But at the beginning of my fourth year at the theater, I looked around and said, "Wait a minute. Here's a theater manager, and he's only making $165 a week and working seventy or eighty hours a week."

In the theater business, you work long hours, and it's hard to have a family. You work weekends and all the holidays, because that's when people go to the movies.

So I decided to go back to school. I took night courses and extra classes and graduated only a semester behind my original class. After I graduated, I became a draftsman. I spent the next twenty-eight years as a supermarket designer. I worked for A&P for ten years and Affiliated Food Stores for eighteen years. It was an eight-to-five job. That's what I liked about it.

But I guess my four years at the theater were my fondest years because of the friends I made there. They were my only friends.

And Interstate had a way of making you proud to be part of the Interstate family. We were proud to be ushers. We were proud of the Interstate Theaters and their first-run movies. We were proud to make our customers comfortable so they could enjoy the movie.

In 1962 or '63, the government said you couldn't have a monopoly and only give the first-run movies to certain theaters. You had to offer them to everybody. That's when suburban theaters started getting first-run releases. The big first-run theaters started going downhill. The whole Interstate system went down.

The Majestic closed in 1973. The last movie to show there was *Live and Let Die*. I really believe that's when downtown Dallas lost a lot of its luster and glamour.

Tony Zoppi was once an advance man for Lyndon Johnson. In addition, Zoppi booked acts for the Riviera Hotel in Las Vegas for seventeen years and collected much memorabilia from that time, some of which is on the wall behind him. Courtesy *The Dallas Morning News*, John F. Rhodes, photographer.

Tony Zoppi

*Tony Zoppi, seventy-nine, displays an
autographed record album on his coffee table.
The inscription reads, "Tony, Thanks for the
start." It's signed, "Tony Bennett." On the
walls are photos of Mr. Zoppi with Bob Hope,
Sammy Davis Jr., Frank Sinatra, Milton
Berle, Louis Armstrong . . .*

I was raised in a town called Long Branch on the Jersey shore.
Lovely little town. When I was in my teens, I went to work at a
very elegant beach club as a page boy. In those days, they didn't
have microphones, so if a guest got a phone call, I would go around
paging him. I worked for tips and loved it.

On weekends, they brought in the Abe Lyman Orchestra, a big
band. Al Logan was the vocalist. Also a guy named Barry Wood,
who was later on the Lucky Strike Hit Parade. Through them I
was able to get the job as band boy in addition to my other job.

I would work from eight to four, when the swimming was going on, and then come back at eight o'clock at night. They had
people like Sophie Tucker and Milton Berle and Martha Raye and
Georgie Jessel. All major names in those days.

I loved being around those people. I knew the entertainers came
in every Thursday afternoon at two o'clock, so I would make it a
point to be out front and carry their bags up to the dressing rooms.
I got to know them that way. I knew that's where I wanted to be.
In show business. I didn't want to be an entertainer. I wanted to
be a writer like Walter Winchell or Ed Sullivan, or maybe an agent
or a manager.

I went to college at Uppsala College and Monmouth College,
and then I was drafted. Before they could draft me, I enlisted. It

was right after Pearl Harbor. God, everybody couldn't wait to run down and enlist. If you didn't, you felt very guilty.

I put in for officers school and got my commission. They sent me to New Orleans, where they were organizing a big general hospital to go overseas. Nine months later, we were sent to Longview, Texas, to train at Harmon Hospital.

While I was there, I did a show for my colonel's birthday. It worked out real well. The commanding officer of Harmon Hospital turned to my commanding officer and said, "I'm looking for a special service officer. Could you transfer that man?" I wasn't that great a soldier, so my colonel said, "Take him."

I really found my niche there. I booked USO shows. I wrote a radio show that we did on KWKH in Shreveport. I went through the wards looking for soldiers who had been shot up or who had come in from the Pacific with some tropical disease. If I found one who had a good story, I would write a script and we would dramatize it. It went over very well.

I met my wife, Terion Hebisen, in Longview. Her husband had been killed on Guadalcanal. She had two babies. About a year later, we were married and I adopted the children, who were four and five. I was really the only father they ever knew.

I got severe kidney hemorrhages and was discharged from the Army. We had to decide whether to go back to New Jersey or stay in Texas. In the meantime, my father had died, my sister had married and moved to California and my mother had gone to live with them. There was no reason to go back to Long Branch. My wife had a little home in Longview, so we stayed.

The *Longview News Journal* offered me a job as sports editor, which meant I covered the City Hall in the morning, the county courthouse in the afternoon, the Chamber of Commerce meeting about four o'clock, and then if there was a ball game at night, I covered the ball game.

One day in 1948, the editor sent me to Canton to cover a speech by Lyndon Johnson, who was running for the Senate. I said, "I've never covered a political speech." The editor said, "Just write it like it was a football game."

Johnson liked my story so much he asked the editor to loan me to him to do his advance publicity. I joined him in Waco. He was in his hotel suite, sitting at his desk in his pajamas. He had his glasses down on his nose, looking at me. I said, "Congressman, I'm Tony Zoppi." He jumped up and grabbed me so hard he almost knocked me over.

Four men were sitting on the couch. They were Felix McKnight of the *Dallas News*, Amon Carter Jr. of the *Fort Worth Star-Telegram*, one of the Hobbys from Houston, and somebody from Austin. Four of the top managing editors in Texas. Johnson told them, "This is the most colorful writer I've seen since Scotty Reston." I didn't know who Scotty Reston was.

Johnson was campaigning in a helicopter, and he wanted me to ride around in it with him. Like an idiot, I said, "Congressman, I don't fly." The minute I said it, I wanted to die. Those four managing editors nearly fell off the couch.

Johnson said, "Travel by train then, and stay twelve hours ahead of me." I went all over Texas, writing advance stories. As a result, I got a job at the *Dallas News*. Felix hired me as a sportswriter.

I worked at that for two years, but I let it be known that I really wanted to write a nightclub column. We had a marvelous nightclub writer named Fairfax Nesbitt, but she hated the job because she couldn't drive. She had to take a cab everywhere.

TV was just beginning and Fairfax asked John Rosenfield, the arts editor, if she could be the television editor. He agreed and put me into nightclubs. I covered shows all over town.

I gave Tony Bennett his first major write-up. In 1953. He had it reprinted in *Variety*. He always says I gave him his start. Later, when he was about to make his debut at the Copa in New York, he sent plane tickets to me and my wife, and we went. He was a sensation. He went straight up from there.

He started bringing me to New York and Chicago and Holly-wood. I became like his good-luck charm. Other people started flying me around the country to their performances. Sometimes I would cover their performances. Sometimes I would just go and spend a couple of days.

I was with the *Dallas News* for fifteen years. Then I went out to Las Vegas to cover Debbie Reynolds at the Riviera Hotel. I had covered many openings in Las Vegas. Frank Sinatra. The Rat Pack. I crossed paths with Sinatra many times. Knew him for thirty-five years. He had a volatile personality. Lots of highs and lows. But he was never anything but gracious to me. A pussycat.

Anyway, while I was there for Debbie, the hotel people asked me if I knew of anyone who would like to have their publicity and public relations job. Just kiddingly, I said, "How about me?" The guy said, "You're exactly what we want. What's your salary?" I told him and they tripled it. Before I left, they tripled that. I had become entertainment director. The last act I booked was Dolly Parton for $350,000 a week. In 1982.

I was at the Riviera for seventeen years. I found an act by the name of Engelbert Humperdinck that nobody knew. He became, at the time, the hottest thing in town. Same thing with Kenny Rogers and Olivia Newton John and Liza Minnelli. And Shirley MacLaine. And Dean Martin. They were clawing their way up. We would put them in as an opening act, and if they did well, we would move them up to headliner.

I left the Riviera because my wife was terminally ill and Las Vegas was changing. I don't think it has changed for the better. The last time I was there, it took thirty minutes to go six blocks. Bumper to bumper to bumper. And what they've done to the Riviera is absolutely criminal. It was the most elegant hotel in Las Vegas. Now it has a pizza parlor and a hamburger joint in it.

I came back to Dallas and went to work for the Fairmont Hotel for two years, then opened my own public relations agency. I booked all of Mary Kay's functions, the Byron Nelson golf tournament, the Yellow Rose Gala. All huge events. I only booked big acts. It was very lucrative.

I was hired every year to book the Red Cross gala in Monte Carlo, one of Princess Grace's great causes. They would call me three months before and tell me who they wanted. Of course, they wanted Sinatra. Well, I knew Frank, and I knew his secretary. Everything went through his secretary. You didn't approach Frank head-on. It took a little doing, but Frank agreed to do the gala.

Before I flew to Monaco to join him, I went to Ferrara's in Little Italy and bought a huge box of Italian pastries and took them with me. When I went into the rehearsal hall, I handed Frank the box and he said, "Oh, my God. I've been dying for something like this. I can't get a decent plate of spaghetti in this town." Next day, he called me and said, "That was an awful nice thing you did. I thank you for it." That side of Sinatra was like a little kid.

What all the stars had in common was ego. If you didn't have an ego, you couldn't be a star. Most of them carried an entourage with them who kept telling them how great they were. That was their job, to wait on the star and tell him how great he was.

Eventually, my clients were requesting more and more rock 'n' roll. So I said, "Well, Tony, you've had a good ride." In 1990 I got out of it. Since then, I travel a lot, go to some very nice functions.

Some of the stars, like Tony Bennett and Bob Hope and Vic Damone, still remember me. They keep in touch.

Jennifer Nguyen is vice chair of the Asian American Chamber of Commerce of Greater Dallas. Courtesy *The Dallas Morning News*, Milton Hinnant, photographer.

Jennifer Nguyen

*Jennifer Nguyen, fifty-two, and her family were
among the first wave of refugees to come to the
United States after the fall of South Vietnam.
They now live in Garland, Texas.*

My husband's name is Thomas. His Vietnamese name is Toung.
My Vietnamese name is Bong. When we became American citizens, we chose American first names. It's easier for work-related and social things.

My husband was a colonel in the South Vietnamese air force. I was working in human resources for an American company in Saigon. I had four kids.

In 1975 we were worried about what was going to happen. But I was not aware of the surrender when it came, when the freedom of my country would go so quickly.

On April 22, I was at the office, and my husband sent his driver for me. When I got home, my children were already waiting for me. My husband's driver told me the U.S. military was going to take us to Thailand for a short vacation. We were allowed to take only two pounds of personal belongings per person.

We got to the base about eleven o'clock. In the evening, my husband showed up. He told me that the United States government was helping Vietnamese officers by taking their families for an R&R, so the officers would be free to fight for our freedom.

I bought that story. I don't know why. I guess I was just so scared. I wanted to be somewhere civil, to take my children where they wouldn't have to hear rockets and bombs every day, every night.

We sat there until midnight. We missed so many trips because they were overbooked. The next morning, my husband had to go.

He said he had to fly his mission at ten o'clock.

I was hoping he would just take off his uniform and mix in with us and run away. I wanted him to be there with us.

But he said no, he had the uniform on, and he couldn't do that. He said he must stay and fight for his country. And he just turned his back on us.

The next day I was still there, sitting in the hangar, waiting. About midnight, my husband came back and visited us. A few minutes later, the bus came. It was our turn to get on the airplane. My children said goodbye to my husband, and we took off.

My oldest daughter was six-and-one-half then. My next one was barely six. My next one was three and my only son was nearly eight months. We had been wearing the same clothes for two days. We had no shower.

It was a giant airplane, called a C-130, I think. It had been used to carry the dead and wounded. Blood was all over the seat where I was sitting. There were eighty-two women and children. Only two or three of us could speak English.

We landed in the Philippines at Clark Air Force Base and were told that the Philippines government didn't want us. So we got back on the same airplane. I asked the pilot, "Where are you taking us now?" I was afraid they were flying us to some foreign country to sell us for slavery. I might not ever see my children again.

They took us to a U.S. Air Force base in Thailand. Then they told us they didn't want us in Thailand, either. We had to leave. We got back on the airplane and they took us to Guam. We got there at midnight. They took us from the airport to a place in the jungle.

The U.S. Marines were chopping trees down and trying to clean up the ground. They were putting up little blue camping tents.

My friend was afraid that somebody was going to rape her, but I told her not to worry. For some reason, I believed in those Marines. I told my friend, "These are not animals. These are good people." I don't know why, but I felt so strongly about that.

Every day I looked for news from home to see if my husband made it. I had lost all my suitcases. My legal documents from home, my ID, my work permit from the South Vietnamese government. I lost everything. What we had on our bodies was all we had.

In Vietnam, we gave our babies warm milk or we breast-fed. We never fed them with cold baby formula milk like in America. When the Red Cross got me some milk for my baby, he got really sick. Diarrhea. You name it. He got them all. I guess because the journey was so hard on him. He was two months premature.

He was ill for a long time. My seven-year-old, Linda, was the mother for the other two. She took them to their daily meals, took them to get in line to take a shower. She did everything for me so I could stay inside that tent and take good care of my son.

When we had been there seven days, someone came to my tent and said, "Your husband is here." He was at the bus station, still wearing his flying suit, his boots, his hat. But the rank on his shoulders was no longer there. And no gun.

He had flown his airplane to Utapao, a United States Air Force base in Thailand. When my husband got out of his airplane, the American military saluted him and said, "Sir, you are no longer an officer. I'm sorry, but you have to take off your rank and your gun right now." And they were already erasing the South Vietnamese flag from the side of the airplane.

It was really painful for my husband, and for me, too. We felt insulted. But we no longer had a country.

After a couple of days, they took us to Camp Pendleton, California. My husband wrote a letter to Major Larry Johnson, his previous instructor at Williams Air Force Base in Arizona, letting him know we were in the United States. Within a week, Major Johnson came to Camp Pendleton to visit with a big trailer full of clothes and food and other things for my family and for other refugees as well. One day at the office we received a phone call. Larry had found a sponsor willing to take my family. That was a miracle phone call.

Rocky Ford was a district manager for an automobile business. He and his wife Roseanne and their teenage daughter Kathy were willing to take us in.

They lived in Mesa, Arizona. They were so generous. They took us home. Several of their friends were waiting to welcome us. They cooked us a big dinner. Meatloaf. But I couldn't eat it. The tomato sauce reminded me of the blood that I sat on in the airplane that brought me out of Vietnam. Twenty-five years later, I still can't eat tomato sauce.

Rocky and Roseanne put us in a room that was even nicer than our home in Saigon. They had baby toys and a bear for my son. Disposable diapers. Even bathing suits for my little girls. That afternoon, Kathy took them to the swimming pool. They jumped into the pool just like American children.

We are American citizens now. We were in Arizona for eleven years. My husband went back to school at Arizona State University and became a chemical engineer. In 1985 he had a job offer from Varo, an electronics company in Garland.

I work for Zurich American Insurance. I am vice chair of the Asian American Chamber of Commerce of Greater Dallas. My children are all married and working. My son Thomas is the only Asian police officer for the city of Garland. I have six grandchildren and another arriving soon.

We could not have all that we have without the American people and the American government. The American people are the most generous people in the whole wide world. Your hearts are open.

Lois Adair, owner, business manager, and waitress at Adair's Saloon, outside her establishment in Deep Ellum. Courtesy *The Dallas Morning News*, Allison V. Smith, photographer.

Lois Adair

Lois Adair, sixty-one, is the proprietor of Adair's Saloon at 2624 Commerce St. in Dallas. Her place is famous for its fat cheeseburgers, its jukebox full of country oldies and the graffiti on the walls.

My father-in-law started the business in '62. My husband, R. L., and I worked for him a couple of years in the late '60s, and when he retired we bought him out in '77. That was over on Cedar Springs. We moved over here in Deep Ellum in '82.

We were leasing the building on Cedar Springs from my father-in-law, and he sold it. We moved to Deep Ellum before Deep Ellum was Deep Ellum. There was nothing down here except us.

We were here a couple of years before anything started happening. If our clientele hadn't followed us from Cedar Springs, we would have starved. The more Deep Ellum developed, the better it got.

R. L. died in '87. I've had it by myself since then. I love it more than anything I've ever done.

I work the night shift, waiting tables. The people in here at night are out to have fun. That makes my job fun, too. There's no way I could sit at a computer nine to five, five days a week. To me, that would be boring. The only thing I don't like about my job is that at 2:15 I have to take up everybody's beer, and some of them aren't finished with it yet. They think I'm a meanie. I have to do it, though.

I've met a lot of nice people. Real neat people from all walks of life. They come in to shoot pool, visit with their friends, listen to the band or the jukebox.

What makes Adair's a special place is all the different kinds of people who come in. You may be in your tux, just come from a wedding, and you may be shooting shuffleboard against some-body in cutoff jeans who's been out at the pool all day. Everybody fits in. Most clubs go for one kind of clientele or another. But for them to all mix in together ... well, it's real strange, but they all do here.

We try to make everybody feel at home. I've had a lot of girls tell me this is where they come if they're going to be by them-selves because they know that nobody's going to mess with them. They don't come in to get picked up, they come in to have a good time.

It's just one big family. It doesn't matter what your occupation is or what you drive or how many credit cards you've got in your pockets. I think our customers feel that.

Another thing I've heard people say is that they can come here and lay their money on the bar and go shoot pool or shuffleboard and come back, and they know their money's still going to be on the bar. They know the bartender's not going to pick it up.

I prefer working the night shift. In the daytime, people come in and eat lunch and go back to work. At night, they come and stay. It's more fun. Plus, I never have to set my alarm clock. I set my alarm clock for years, and I'm so glad I don't have to do that any-more.

Whenever I get up in the morning, which is anywhere from 9:30 to eleven, I do yesterday's books, make my phone calls and run my errands. Then I take a nap. Then I come to work about nine-thirty or ten at night and stay here till we close. Up until about two years ago, I came to work at six and worked until two and still did all my taking care of business before I got here. But I can't do that anymore.

Everything gets old, I guess. For years, the jukebox man had been wanting me to get rid of my old 45-rpm jukebox and change to a CD jukebox. I didn't want to do it. He finally promised that if I would put in a CD jukebox, he would get me all the oldies I had on 45s.

I think the only song we don't have that we had on the old one is "Happy Trails" by Roy Rogers. We've got "Long Black Veil" by Lefty Frizzell. We've still got Hank Williams and Ernest Tubb and Webb Pierce and Patsy Cline and Jimmie Rodgers. I still have, oh, what's his name? Eddie Arnold. "Cattle Call." Yeah. They're all still on there.

It just amazes me how young people in their twenties can come in and sing along with, say, Hank Williams or Bob Wills. I mean, those guys were gone before these kids were even born. It's neat that their music has lived on. And with the CD jukebox, I have room to put on some of the new stuff recorded by the bands that play in here. That's the main reason I changed.

Very, very seldom do I have a problem with a customer. The gang that shoots pool hangs out in the back. It's their place to play, and they're not going to cause any problems. Another group sits up at the very front and listens to the band all night. They may be as regular as the ones in the back, but they probably don't even know each other.

Any time there's trouble—any time—it's always an outsider. Usually you can spot the guy when he comes in. I guess it's because I've been in the business so long. I think, "You know, I need to keep an eye on that person."

The last time we had trouble with a guy, the bartender was thinking, "You know, I probably should put that person out, because we're going to have trouble with him." And I was thinking the same thing. But we didn't say anything to each other. Sure enough, after the problem we had, we got to talking and found out we were thinking the same thing.

I don't know what it is about troublemakers, but you can spot them. Anybody who has worked in a bar any length of time can pretty much tell you that. Isn't that strange?

People are always telling me they would like to own a bar, but they're in front of the bar when they were talking, not behind it. They don't know the work involved.

The only way to run a successful business is hands-on. You're more or less married to the bar. I work seven days a week. One thing that makes it so hard is that I'm doing it alone now. When R. L. was alive, we would share the work and the responsibility. Now it's all mine.

I'm closed on Sunday, but I'm still doing books, inventory, time sheets, whatever. When I go to Tyler to visit my mother, I take my books to work on while I'm there. The only place I don't take my work with me is when I go visit my grandchildren. They live in Meridian, Texas. I never take work down there. I'll just be behind when I get back.

People ask me when I'm going to retire. I have no plans to do that. This place has been my life too long. What would I do without it?

Clebo Rainey is one of the best known performance poets in the country. Here he is at his regular Friday night gig at Club Clearview in Dallas. Courtesy *The Dallas Morning News*, Damon Winter, photographer.

Clebo Rainey

Every Friday night for five years, performance poet Clebo Rainey, fifty, has been conducting poetry slams, in which poets compete for prize money, at Club Clearview in Deep Ellum. His wife, Noemi Collie, is a lawyer specializing in employment discrimination and civil rights. She makes the living.

I grew up in a little place called Pine Springs about twelve miles outside of Tyler in the East Texas Piney Woods. My grandfather on my mom's side drove an eighteen-wheeler for years and died driving one. He was changing a tire and the tire rolled out and broke his shoulder. He fell down an embankment and had a heart attack and froze to death.

My grandfather on my father's side was a wildcatter who drilled oil wells all over the world. My grandmother wanted to honky-tonk with him and travel around the world, so she stuck her five sons and her daughter in an orphans home when they were all teenagers, and just left them there.

When World War II came along, my dad ran away and lied about his age and joined the Navy. He put himself through college after that with the GI Bill. He became a printer, and eventually became an industrial graphic artist and settled in Tyler.

When I was in the fifth grade, they gave us all an aptitude test to find out what we should be good at. Mine was music, so they stuck a French horn in my hand and from the fifth grade on I played in the band. I was a drum major in high school. I also got into acting. It was a toss-up whether I was going to be an actor or a musician, but I went to Tyler Junior College and majored in music. I intended to become a high school band director.

Then I went to SMU. That was in '69. That was, like, Kent State, Vietnam, civil rights protests. I got totally caught up in all of that. My dad was kind of a bigot, a Nixon guy, a Republican, and I was a long-haired hippie freak. Like a lot of kids in my generation, that pretty much destroyed my relationship with my family.

My dad died about fifteen years ago. At the time, we weren't on speaking terms. My parents were always disowning me, and we would go for years without talking. Then they would call me up and say, "Oh, we really miss you." I would go visit them, but I was still a weird artist, so they would disown me again.

That cycle went on and on until my dad dropped dead at sixty while taking a shower. He smoked three packs of cigarettes a day and had heart problems.

Now my mom and I speak. She comes for Christmas and we fix breakfast for her and we exchange $50 gifts and that's about it. I've got a sister who's like real religious and my mom's total little pet. She's a big hard-core Baptist. But now that I'm pretty well-known and travel around the country and have a nice house and am married to a lawyer, I'm a little more acceptable.

I was in my sixth year of college and six weeks away from getting my teaching certificate when I and a bunch of other students took over the SMU administration building. It was the day after Kent State. We barricaded ourselves and put a big banner out the window with a red fist on it that said, "Strike." There were even some teachers in there with us. It was crazy, but, for God's sake, they were killing students at Kent State!

Suddenly, we were surrounded by about 500 Dallas sheriffs who came to get out about 100 students. They just took our names and let us go. But a few nights later they had what we called the SMU Massacre, where they went out and busted about forty of those students for drugs. Everyone at SMU was doing drugs, but they busted just those who had been in the strike.

I was working at Bank AmeriCard at night and I had three music scholarships, one because I was a poor kid going to SMU, and the others because I was in the marching band and the jazz band and the wind ensemble. I was a valve trombone player.

I came home from my job at Bank AmeriCard at One Main Place about nine o'clock one night. As I was about to turn on my lamp, two plainclothes policemen grabbed me and started whaling on me. I didn't know who they were. I started fighting back. Suddenly they turned the light on, and they had me by my hair and they had a gun at my throat. And they go, "This is a bust! Federal indictment! Fight back, you hippie pig! We'd love to blow your head off!" It was crazy.

It was the first time I had ever been arrested in my life. The last time, for that matter. They handcuffed me and put me in a police car and took me down to the University Park police station.

That was the first time my parents disowned me. Then the dean of men called me and said, "You can't get a teaching certificate while you're under federal indictment." I was kicked out of school. I couldn't work in a bank while I was under federal indictment, either, so I got fired.

My lawyer said so many rich kids were getting busted for drugs there was no way they were going to be sent to prison. He thought there soon would be a change in the law, so he kept putting my case off until that happened.

I hitchhiked around the country for about a year, and then came back and plea-bargained two years' probation and a $5,000 fine. While I was on probation, I worked at Doubleday Books downtown and was eventually transferred out to NorthPark, where I was paperback buyer.

After I got off probation, I went to Denver and worked there and met my first wife, Babs. We came back to Dallas and started a record shop, Metamorphosis Records, in the early '70s. And we had the Metamorphosis Concert Hall, the second New Wave club in Dallas. I played guitar and saxophone and valve trombone, and we had this band called Point of Departure that was a kind of electronic jazz-rock dance band. We worked at that for fifteen years.

When I was about thirty-six, I had a midlife-crisis period. I left my wife, Babs, for this young girl, Laura, that I met. The same night I met her, I met a theater company called the Theater of All Possibilities at the Caravan of Dreams in Fort Worth. It was kind of a theater-cult thing. I wound up touring with them. I rode a motorcycle out to the West Coast, where I met Lawrence Ferlinghetti, Timothy Leary, William Burroughs and Allen Ginsberg.

One day I rode my motorcycle up to the overlook on Mulholland Drive, where L.A. is spread out below you. While I was up there, I wrote a poem called "L.A. Stretched Out." That was my first poem. I realized right away that it was really good. To this day, it's one of my best poems. People request it all the time.

Then I went down to Beverly Hills and wrote another poem called "A Ballad of a Wayward Husband." I read it to my theater friends, and they said, "Wow! That's good!" So I kept writing.

The play wound up in Austin, and I met some people there who were poets. That's all they did. They were poets. So by the time I pulled back into Dallas on my motorcycle after this 6,000-mile journey, my first two thoughts were: "My God, I've survived!" and "I'm going to be a poet! That's what I want to do with the rest of my life!"

I moved out by White Rock Lake to a little $200-a-month garage apartment. I parked my bike and got a little part-time job and reinvented myself. I gave up the hard drugs, gave up the sixteen- and seventeen-year-old girls, gave up the really, really bad ways that have since killed several friends of mine, and for a year I just stayed by the lake and wrote poems.

Then a lesbian friend of mine brought Noemi Collie out. Noemi wanted to hire me to read poetry at her New Year's Eve party. I fixed her some hot tea and played my guitar for her and read her some poetry, and it was love at first sight. She was everything I had been waiting for. We had one date that never ended. Within a week, she was moving in.

I wrote a poem on her body, which is called "A Poem for Her Flesh," and that was the title of my first book, which is poems about women.

Noemi and I made a deal at the beginning that she was going to be the major breadwinner and have her law practice, and I would be a poet full time and do all the housework, cleaning, cooking, all of which I do to this day, ten years later.

I travel around the country a lot, doing about forty gigs in forty-five days around fifteen or more states and up into Canada. I do East Coast tours, West Coast tours, middle-of-the-country tours. I do poetry slams, art galleries, coffeehouses, bars, colleges, high schools. On a good tour, I'll come home with about $1,000 in my pocket. That's after expenses.

When I'm writing, I use sex, drugs or rock 'n' roll to work myself into a certain state, and then I write as fast as I possibly can. I go back later and edit out a few "ands" and "thats," but mostly when I write it down, it's done. Boom. I try to capture that moment that I'm in and the idea that I've had in that moment.

I've written five books that have twenty-five poems apiece in them. Those are my keeper poems. I've got another book I'm ready to write, so there's twenty-five more. That's 150 keepers. For every keeper poem I write, there are about three poems that aren't keepers. So over the years, I guess I've written about 600 poems.

A keeper has to have an idea that kind of permeates the piece and good imagery and a uniqueness to it. Writers know what that they do is first-rate and what's second-rate. They can tell when something they write has everything. There's no better feeling than that.

Jeanette Crumpler in her back yard in East Dallas holding some of her home-grown tomatoes. She said her gardening helps her deal with the death of her two sons. Courtesy *The Dallas Morning News*, David Woo, photographer.

Jeanette Crumpler

For more than three decades, the residents of her Lakewood neighborhood in East Dallas have called Jeanette Crumpler, sixty-six, the Tomato Lady because of her pleasure in sharing her garden's generous yield.

I've always loved gardening. I've done it since I was a child. My boys enjoyed it, too. They would join me out in the big vegetable garden I had in the back yard.

It's a neat thing to go out there now and enjoy what they liked. I always plant sunflowers and tomatoes and things that they enjoyed planting, too. It's not only a comfort, it's kind of a renewing thing. It makes me feel good to go out there and realize how beautiful this world is, despite its trials and sorrows and heartaches.

They tell me I was about three years old when I became a gardener. I grew up in Wichita Falls. We moved there from Oklahoma when I was three months old, and we bought a house in 1936, when I was three years old. My dad put in a big vegetable garden, because those days in the '30s, if you didn't garden, you didn't eat.

My dad was a lawyer who had lost a business in Oklahoma during the Depression and had the equivalent of a nervous breakdown and went to work in the county clerk's office. He gardened. He loved to garden. It was his therapy. He would just get out there and dig in the dirt.

They tell me that when I was about three, I would follow my dad and my grandmother out to the garden in the morning. They said I wanted to know everything about the plants, the names of them and all that. So I grew up gardening in the back yard.

My dad was a good one for the vegetables and flowers, and my grandmother grew herbs.

Her father had been a surgeon during the Civil War, and when they came to Texas in the 1870s, she became his nurse. They made a lot of their medicines with the herbs that she grew, as well as the chemicals that he ordered from a pharmaceutical house in Chicago. So she always talked about the benefits of herbal medicines along with other medicines. She grew herbs of every kind, and I wanted to know the names of all of them and what they were good for.

My dad and my grandmother would get mad at each other and wouldn't talk to each other, but they would work at opposite ends of the garden, and I had my little patch in the middle.

Other than the years when I was discovering boys and dating, I've always gardened.

I moved into this house in 1960. I was married and had the two boys. I put in a vegetable garden, and I've been here ever since.

For thirty years, I did seed trials for companies. The National Gardening Association test panel wanted test gardeners for the home back yard. I wrote them. They had about 5,000 applicants, and they chose 200 of them to do seed trials.

I trialed about 300 varieties of tomatoes. I raised a lot of tomatoes. I gave away lots and lots of tomatoes and tomato plants. I got to be known around here as the Tomato Lady.

In this part of Texas, the hybrids work best. First, you have to amend the soil. You have to add a lot to it. And if you grow the seedlings yourself, they're usually healthier. The hybrids have more disease resistance. Like President and Super Fantastic and Celebrity and Sweet 100.

The main problems in Texas are early blight and red spiders. I'm an organic gardener, pretty much. I don't spray. I plant trap plants around the tomatoes. The insects are attracted to them and eat them instead of the tomato plants.

My garden is not the square, green kind. It's kind of jungley, but it sure produces stuff.

I was divorced in '73 and kept the house. Then my oldest boy went into the service and was gone. And my deaf son, the younger son, went to the Texas School for the Deaf. So he was gone. I kept shrinking down the size of my garden. Now it's not real big, but it's still producing good tomatoes.

This year I have about twelve tomato plants, I have some beans, I have some peppers and cucumbers, and lots of flowers and herbs, and a few stray stalks of corn.

My oldest boy, Bruce, died in 1979 as the result of injuries from an automobile accident. He was twenty-six. He was about to get married. He and his fiancée had met in the Air Force.

She's still like a daughter to me. It's been twenty years, and we're still just as close. She's my heir. I don't have any other family. She married a sweet young man and had two sweet girls. They live in Indiana now. They bring their girls and come to see me. I'm kind of like their Texas aunt.

My other son, Dean, was born deaf. I had Asiatic flu when I was carrying him, and they gave me tetracycline for it. At the time, there was no warning about it affecting a baby. There was so much they didn't know. He was born brain-damaged. He had a lot of problems. He died of a terminal disease in '93. He was thirty-five.

I don't know why gardening is such good therapy for grieving people. Maybe it's our connection with the earth. I'm a Christian, so I believe the Lord himself did design that first environment for us. And it was a garden. I think we're still connected with the earth and what it produces. It renews your faith in life going on.

Whatever it is, it's perfectly enjoyable and stimulating. I just get a kick out of going out there and looking at the garden and what's growing. Beans, butterflies, birds. Not to mention the food that it produces. It's just a miracle how those little seeds produce all this good food.

If you get to a child young enough and teach him how to garden, then it never leaves him.

I also grow a lot of herbs. Different kinds of basil, bay, sage, several different kinds of rosemary, mint, cilantro, parsley, verbena, oregano. I grow cucumbers, some corn, beans.

And flowers. I have some perennials that are doing real well right now, before the grasshoppers and the worms get to them. If something gets blight, I just let it go. I have some morning glories.

The garden is smaller now than it used to be. When the boys were growing up, it went clear to the back fence.

I always plant sunflowers in memory of the boys. They used to have a sunflower race every year. I would give them the seeds and they would plant them and see whose sunflower would grow the tallest.

Frank Rush, Sr., owner of Sandy Lake Park, and a portrait of his father, Frank S. Rush. Courtesy *The Dallas Morning News*, Allison V. Smith, photographer.

Frank Rush

*Frank Rush is eighty-four. Nearly his whole life
has been spent in the entertainment and
amusements business. Since 1969, he and his
family have owned and operated Sandy Lake
Amusement Park in Carrollton, Texas.*

I was born in 1915 on the Wichita Mountains Wildlife Refuge
near Cache, Oklahoma. The refuge was one of the first national
parks that Teddy Roosevelt created in 1907. At that time it was
under the supervision of the Forest Service. My daddy was one of
the men who started the buffalo herd there.

The buffalo were pretty well gone from the plains. Roosevelt
and some others got the idea of getting some of the buffalo out of
the New York Zoological Park and putting them in those mountains. They contacted Pawnee Bill, who had a famous Wild West
show, to recommend somebody to do it. He recommended my
father, Frank Rush, who was running a ranch in the Osage Nation.

So he went to New York and got fifteen buffalo. They loaded
them in crates and Daddy rode the train with them to Cache. Then
they loaded them on a caravan of wagons and hauled them to the
refuge. They arrived in the Wichita Mountains on October 18, 1907.
Before I was born. Since then, they've reproduced thousands of
descendants who have gone to zoos and parks all over the world.

The great cattleman Charlie Goodnight and Pawnee Bill and
Daddy started cross-breeding buffalo with cattle. They called the
result "cattalo." They wrote back and forth when they were doing
that, and by doing so they became very well acquainted. When I
was two or three or four years old, Charlie Goodnight came to our
house. I have a picture somewhere of me sitting on his knee.

Mother and I stayed at Pawnee Bill's house many a night. I called him Uncle Bill. Daddy knew Buffalo Bill real well, too, and the Miller Brothers, who had the famous 101 Ranch Wild West show. The ranch that Daddy was on before he came to the refuge adjoined the Miller Brothers'. I saw the final performance of their show on Labor Day 1928, I think it was. I was about twelve years old.

Quanah Parker was a close friend of Daddy's. Quanah and the Indians were there when they unloaded the buffalo. I'm pretty sure that Daddy was a pallbearer at Quanah Parker's funeral. I know he was a pallbearer when they brought Cynthia Ann Parker's remains from Texas back to Oklahoma. She died in Texas in 1870 and was brought back to Oklahoma in 1910.

So I was born there on the refuge. After the buffalo were established, Daddy retired and bought some land north of Cache and started a park. We called it Craterville Park. It had a skating rink and a campground. That's where I became six or seven years old and went to school.

In 1927, when I was about twelve years old, J. Frank Dobie and others started the longhorn herd at the Wichita Mountains refuge. I saw them unload those cattle off of railroad cars at Cache. There were thirty-seven of them, I think. They drove them to our park and put them in our rodeo arena for the night. I can still hear them bawl. The next day, they drove them up to the refuge headquarters.

We've always been in entertainment. I love it.

We had our park in Oklahoma for forty-six years. Over the years it grew into a dude ranch with cabins, grocery stores, a hotel, restaurants. I lost my father when I was seventeen. He passed away of a stroke. That fall, Genelle and I married. I started to college, but the park was there, and Mother was by herself. So we ran the park.

We had acts come out from Nashville and had a free show on our stage every Saturday and Sunday. Roy Acuff, Minnie Pearl, all those. People would come and camp and be entertained. In those days, people would put up tents and sleep on cots. There was no air conditioning.

We worked with Walt Disney and others, making movies about the buffalo. They used our horses. Then Mike Todd came along and used the buffalo in *Around the World in 80 Days*. We were very successful in boarding them, making them box lunches, taking care of their people. It was good business for us.

We started an Indian store on old 62 Highway. We had a merry-go-round and stuff. Kind of a tourist trap on the highway. Mother looked after that.

In 1956, the Army at Fort Sill condemned about 200,000 acres for a firing range. Our 4,700-acre dude ranch was part of that. So we were out. We bought a ranch north of the mountains and lived there ten years. We raised quarter horses and Herefords. Our two kids went through high school and college.

Mother passed away in 1966. She died of leukemia.

We had done rodeos all over Oklahoma. In our rodeos there was more trick riding, trick roping, more circus-type things than they do now. Times were different. Trick roping and trick riding are pretty well lost arts now. I trick-roped twenty years. Mrs. Rush had a dressage horse that she used, and we done those rodeos in southwestern Oklahoma and North Texas.

Six Flags Over Texas started in 1965. In 1966, Mr. Angus Wynn, who built Six Flags, contacted me. He said, "They tell me you produce Western shows." I said I did. I learned it from my father and Pawnee Bill. Mr. Wynn said, "I want a Western show with flags and pretty girls and a stagecoach. You know, something nice. Quality. Pretty. Something Texas." I said, "Well, that's easy done."

In the beginning, we had Indians, which we could get then from Oklahoma. We had the six flags. We had Spanish and French and Texas and so forth. And we brought in an act with each flag. America was trick riders. Texas was a stagecoach holdup. And so on.

Mr. H. L. Hunt used to ride in the stagecoach sometimes. He loved it. And the Cuellar brothers, who owned El Chico. They were lovely people. I was at Mother Cuellar's funeral. And so forth. Angus Wynn came down and said, "I just love this. We'll do this from now on." And I thought, "Well, that's a pretty long time."

Anyhow, we were there two years. We lived there, in the middle of Six Flags. We had about thirty-five show people and about fifty head of horses.

Then I saw this place. Sandy Lake Park. It was just an old swimming pool, in pretty bad shape, and a miniature golf course. It was closed. Its reputation wasn't very good. In 1969 we moved here.

We've been here twenty-nine years. We've always catered to families. We started with the merry-go-round, bumper cars, train and picnics. Our family's all here. We all live on the grounds.

We started out small. Now we have nineteen American-made rides, twenty-two picnic areas. Paddle boats. Ball fields. We get a lot of family reunions, company groups, church groups. We have 100 acres of land.

We have enough. We haven't wanted to get over our head. It's all paid for. We don't owe anything. We pay as we go.

And it has worked. We're affordable. We're clean. We're shade trees and green grass, basically. Originally, that's what parks were. Picnic parks.

We're very happy here. Soon Genelle and I will celebrate our 66th wedding anniversary. Lord, have we been blessed, to live in the times that we have.

Instructor Denise Brown straightens the posture of one of her students at City Ballet. Ms. Brown participated in the French Resistance during WWII. Courtesy *The Dallas Morning News*, Natalie Caudill, photographer.

Denise Brown

Denise Brown was born in Paris in 1925. During World War II she was active in the French Underground. Since coming to this country as a war bride she has taught ballet to generations of Dallas children.

I came from a nice family. My father, Sadi Lattes, was an engineer. He and my mother were both musicians. They did living-room concerts to entertain us. Music was in our home, always.

I introduced dancing to the family. Ballet. They didn't think it was quite an art. Respectable girls didn't dance for a living. But when I was a little girl I was scrawny and the doctor recommended exercise for me. So I took dance lessons for that reason. That made it OK.

In the '30s, my parents sent me to England to learn English. That was a custom in my family. As we grew older, we were supposed to go to different countries and spend a summer there and pick up a bit of the language. Of course, the war put a stop to that.

My father was an officer in the army reserve and had gone to the front. My mother and my brother—he's three years younger than I—moved to the Riviera and lived at first with my grandparents in Nice.

Then we went to an old house our family had owned for four generations. It's close to the Spanish border, almost in the Pyrenees. During the war it was a rendezvous for our family. Everybody said, "If anything happens and you get cut off, go to Bousquet d'Orb or get in touch with whoever will be there." That was the name of the little town. "Orb" means "tree" and "bousquet" means "forest." It means "forest of trees."

My great-grandfather, who was a mining engineer, started that little town. He had sixteen living children. He had so many heirs. My grandmother got her part, and so did a million of her cousins. By the time it got to my mother, it was just crazy. There were 172 heirs to the house. It still belongs to some members of the family, but my mother sold her part of it.

We went there. Everybody else in the family went there or sent word. For three miserable months, 132 of us were living in that house. Five generations. Food was a problem. We kids bicycled all up and down those mountains, trying to locate a little butter or a little cheese.

After France surrendered, we finally heard from my father. He was through with the army. He wanted us to come back to Paris. We got there at the end of July or the beginning of August in 1940.

Life in Paris was sad during the German occupation. The city lost its oomph. We had many curfews. There were no lights. In the winter it's totally dark in Paris by 3:30. It was a sad city.

Finding something to eat became harder and harder. Even if you had ration coupons, there was nothing in the stores to trade them for. We would relay each other, standing in the lines for the milk ration or the sugar ration. I would go early, and then Mother would come take my place when my brother and I had to go to school.

Often they would close the door before she got anything. That was the end for that day. The next day it would start all over. The only things people cared about were finding something to eat and getting rid of the Germans.

My father had gone into the army as a captain and came out as a major. I don't know why he was promoted, because they didn't really fight very long. He was a stubborn, high-strung person. He had his own ideas about the surrender of France. He hated the Vichy government. He felt we had been sold, and he was right.

He was working hard in the Underground, in the Resistance. We didn't know about it. Well, my brother and I weren't supposed to know. We never asked him what he was doing, because the less you knew, the better off you were. But we knew that sometimes he would be gone all day and all night, and he had never traveled in his work before. We didn't have to ask questions. There was a kind of unspoken language that made you know what was going on.

He was part of blowing up the Renault factory, which was working for the Germans. And he was arrested a few days later. In December of '41. Three days before he was arrested, a plane had come from England to pick him up, but there was too much fog and the plane couldn't land.

Mother told us this later on. So he was arrested. And we never heard from him anymore. They sent him to a prison in Germany and he was killed there.

I was sixteen years old, but I decided I would do whatever I could. I was talking with some friends who were a little older than I, and somehow I realized they were working for the Resistance. I went to work for it, too. I was just one of the little people whom they needed a lot of, to take a paper to someone, to take guns down into the mountains, stuff of that sort.

Of course, we never knew any of the higher-ups in our group. We just knew the people we had contact with. We didn't even know them by their last names. We kept our given names, because it was so easy for someone to call you in the street, and you might answer automatically or turn your head.

One time I was supposed to meet somebody in a certain park who would be reading a newspaper. I had a message for him. I was supposed to sit down beside this person and read my newspaper and give him the message. But there were two men there reading newspapers. Which one was it?

Whoever was supposed to contact me didn't know whether I was a girl or a man. The three of us were reading newspapers. I kept waiting for one of them to get up and go. Nothing happened. Finally I got disgusted and put my newspaper in the trash bin and left. I never knew which one was the contact I was supposed to make. I couldn't take a chance.

But you know what? When you're seventeen or eighteen years old, you really don't care. I guess that's why so many young people were in the Resistance. When you're that young, you're fearless. You don't think of all the things that could happen.

After my father was arrested, we stayed in Paris another eight or ten months, but the Germans kept coming to the house and asking questions. My mother decided we should leave. We started moving around the country, not staying long in one spot.

When we were on the loose like that, we didn't have any ration coupons. We had friends who could put one of us up, but not three. So we would split up and stay with whoever was willing to give us a little hot water and a bed.

I think my mother was involved in the Underground, too. She had a brilliant mind. But she wouldn't talk about it after the war.

I was in a town close to Lyon when Paris was liberated. I was working with the Maquis, who were members of the Underground hiding out in the forests and the countryside. They were guerrillas. If you heard that someone had gone into the Maquis, you knew he couldn't be found.

I was helping get guns and ammunition and money and clothes to them. I was engaged to a boy who was in the Maquis. He was killed in December of '43.

Some of us went from farm to farm, trying to feel out the people to see which ones might help the Maquis. Farmers in central France are exceedingly reticent. They're loners. You don't walk in and say, "Hi, how are you?" You have to get to them slowly.

Most of them lived in just one room, but some had lofts where they could hide somebody. It was a remote area. The German army didn't travel through there much. There was a great deal of Underground work going on there.

I had false papers that said I was a student at a secretary school. One day I was walking with an Underground contact of mine, and the Germans tapped us on our shoulders and wanted to see our papers. We both had false papers with false names on them. The Germans took us to the Gestapo headquarters. They made me sit down in the lobby and told me to wait.

I don't know whom to thank for saving my life. The Gestapo called the secretary school and asked if I was registered there. And whoever answered the phone said, "Yes, she's registered here." That wasn't true. But the Gestapo said I could go. I figure I had a good angel that morning.

The Gestapo took my contact away. I never heard from him anymore.

I was in Lyon when it was under heavy bombardment by the Americans. The Americans were smart. They bombed from very high up in the sky. The anti-aircraft shells couldn't reach them. The British came very low. We saw a lot of British planes hit. I would help with the cleanup after the bombardment. It had to be done. We didn't have tools. It was a pointless job. We couldn't save a lot of people, but it gave us the idea that we were trying. It kept us going.

The British bombing was always very accurate. The British trusted the information we gave them. Such as: "There's a red cross on that building, but it isn't a hospital." And the British would come as close as they could to their targets and dive bomb.

But I don't know whether American intelligence always trusted the information sent to them by the French. The Americans sent hundreds of big bombers that we could hear for a long time. They would stay very high, and many times they would miss their targets and hit civilians.

We didn't care, because we knew that was the only way to scat those "boches." That was our name for the Germans. You know, like the Americans called them the "jerries."

I was in Paris, staying at an aunt's house, when Normandy was invaded. There was such panic. We didn't know what was going on. Here would come a whole load of Germans, and they would say, "The Americans are right behind us!" Everybody would pull out their flags and put them in their windows. Then here would come the Germans back, and everybody would hide their flags again. It was a very wild time.

After everything settled down and the American army was in Paris, we were ecstatic. We still didn't have enough to eat, but we weren't under the German boots anymore. That was such a relief that nothing else seemed to matter.

My mother asked me one day, "What are you going to do with your life?" By then I was twenty years old. I wanted to do something for the Americans. They liberated us. We were alive because of them. I knew they needed people who could speak both French and English. I went to their headquarters and applied for a job. I said, "I speak English. Excuse me, I speak British." They thought that was very funny.

A couple of days later I got a call from the 198th General Hospital. They needed a translator for the commanding officer. My job kept blossoming. I did all sorts of things. During the Battle of the Bulge in December of '44 and January of '45, they were bringing in hundreds and hundreds of wounded GIs.

Somebody would run down the hall yelling, "They're bringing in 500 guys!" and the office workers would get off their typewriters and come to help. I was there sometimes until midnight, not translating but helping a poor guy who maybe didn't have his hands or he didn't have his eyes. As they were unloaded off the trucks, I would light cigarettes for them, give them a drink of water, stay with them until the military personnel could take charge of them.

After the Germans collapsed in '45, the 198th General Hospital was going with the Seabees to the Asian war front. I thought, "OK, my good deed for the American army is done. Now I've got to sit down and figure out what I'm going to do with my life." But the Americans still needed somebody at the finance headquarters. I kept telling them I wasn't interested. But I went to work there.

That's where I met my husband, James Eugene Brown. He was an enlisted man in the office next door to where I worked. It wasn't love at first sight. We just started talking, and things went along, and one day he asked me to get married.

He was from a little town called Emhouse, close to Corsicana. He told me Emhouse had 280 population, including chickens and dogs and cats, but that Corsicana was a big, big town. That's where I landed, a pregnant war bride. I stood at one end of Corsicana's main street, which is called Beaton Street. There wasn't a building more than two stories high. I thought, "That's the big town? Where am I?" I think Gene was a little shaken up himself. It was smaller than he remembered.

Anyhow, we landed at Emhouse. My husband's father worked at the gin. We moved in with his parents. They were not happy at all with me. I was a foreigner with a British accent. I asked my mother-in-law what I should call her, and she said, "Mrs. Brown." That's what I called her as long as she was alive.

And there was a picture of a young woman hanging over the bed in the room we were given. When I asked her who it was, she said, "That's the girlfriend Gene should have married."

After three months we moved in with an aunt whose husband had passed away. I was bored to tears in that town. My husband's family was very . . . I wouldn't say "religious," but they thought they were. I had a deck of cards. One 100-degree afternoon, I was going to play solitaire. Mrs. Brown knocked the cards to the floor and said, "There won't be any gambling in my house!"

Gene had managed two years of college before he enlisted. He wanted to go back to school, but we had a new baby and no money. It looked as though it was going to be one of those hopeless things.

But we were good friends with Bill Stewart, the minister of the little Methodist church. He had two or three churches and would come to Emhouse every third week or whatever. He was a student at Perkins School of Theology at SMU.

My daughter Janine was born in Corsicana. "Janine" stands for the "J" in my husband's name. Each of our children was named for a letter in his name. "A" is our second daughter, Anette. "M" is our son, Michael. "E" is for our third daughter, Evelyn. "S" was for "stop," as far as I was concerned.

Bill Stewart talked my husband into going back to school on the GI Bill. I will ever be thankful to him. Because if we talked about that in Emhouse, my husband's family would say, "Oh, you don't need to go to school. You can get a job at the gin."

We lived with Bill and his wife, Jean, and their little child in their Quonset hut at Love Field. It was close living, but they were an absolutely wonderful couple.

We finally found ourselves a one-room garage apartment at a doctor's house. Gene studied in the bathroom so the baby could sleep. He would sit on the john and I would pick up the bridge table and put it across his lap and put two of its legs into the bath-tub. We lived there for eight or nine months. It was OK.

Gene became a CPA and was hired to be the finance director of the city of University Park. He was there thirty-five years, until he retired.

My grandfather had given me a little money when I married. I was determined not to touch it except for something important. The doctor's wife told me about a house for sale on Purdue. We put my money down on it. My husband almost had a stroke, it cost so much. $13,000. But we bought it. Our first home. We had a hard time making the payments. We took in a boarder, an SMU student. Don Brooks. A delightful young man. He stayed with us for two years.

Our next-door neighbor wanted her three daughters to have ballet. I hadn't danced much in France because my parents didn't think it was respectable for a woman to show her ankle, and I would not dance during the German occupation. But my neighbor said, "Why don't you start a little school?"

My studio was our bedroom. Every day I was teaching, I pushed the bed into the hall and put it back after class. I had quite a few kids from the neighborhood and charged $2 a month for two classes a week. I was so happy. It was great to be busy.

By the second year I had fifty students. People in the neighborhood were seeing all those kids coming and going, and somehow word of it got to City Hall. The city manager called in my husband and said, "I understand your wife is running a little business at your home. It would be good if she moved it out."

I moved my studio to Snider Plaza for about a year, then rented a studio on Lovers Lane near Douglas. When that got too small, I moved two blocks west and across the street. When that got too small, I moved three doors down. When the block was sold, I built a studio on Sherry Lane, then moved to an awful shopping center on Walnut Hill. I couldn't find a place I liked and could afford.

A friend, Bourdon Smith, who was a minister at Northaven Methodist Church, invited us to be part of the arts program of the church. We were associated with the church for five years, but again we needed more space. We moved to our present studio in '92, soon after my husband died. Lovers Lane at the Dallas North Tollway. You can see the sign from the Tollway. City Ballet. That's us.

Last year was the 50th anniversary of the school. My daughter Evelyn is co-director with me now. We have about 275 kids. Some of them come four or five times a week. I'm teaching the children and grandchildren of my former students.

You know, life makes you what you are. Sometimes the hardest part of life makes your character. Before the war, I was a nice little French girl with nannies and servants in the home. Soft. The war changed me. It prepared me for the challenge of coming to Texas. It *was* a challenge, let me tell you. But it taught me patience.

Burt Finger is the owner of Photographs Do Not bend, a photographic gallery on Routh Street in Dallas. Courtesy *The Dallas Morning News*, Jim Mahoney, photographer.

Burt Finger

Burt Finger, fifty-five, and his wife, Missy, own
Photographs Do Not Bend, a photography gallery at
3115 Routh Street in Dallas. Work by some of the
world's best art photographers is exhibited there.

I was born on the Lower East Side of New York. A lot of immigrants were there. Italians, Jewish, Irish. An interesting area to live in. When I was seven or eight, my family moved to Brooklyn. I went to junior high school there.

When I was fourteen, my dad was offered a job in Dallas, selling clothing wholesale to department stores. He felt it would be a better place to raise children. I had a sister. He wasn't happy with us living in New York then. Situations that were happening there. People I was involved with.

I've been in Dallas since 1958. I'm a Texan. I mean, I really feel like one, a native Texan. But also part New Yorker.

Imagine leaving the streets of Brooklyn and coming to Dallas. When I left Brooklyn, I thought the whole United States looked like Brooklyn, that it was paved from the East Coast to the West Coast. My vision of Texas was that there were streets like Brooklyn, and then a ranch that went on forever.

When I got here, I was totally amazed. It was truly culture shock. The way I looked, the way I walked, the way I talked were different from here. I might as well have been painted orange. I really stood out. I had a difficult time adjusting.

I went to Thomas Jefferson High School. I had trouble making friends. Most of the friends I did make were people who marched to the beat of a different drummer. They were people who were maybe more studious, interested in art, and not conformists. The conforming part of the high school, the really great-looking girls, the cheerleaders, would have nothing to do with me. I was an aberration. It was difficult. It was a major problem for me.

I graduated in '61 and went to North Texas State University and studied biology. That lasted a semester. I realized all those labs were cutting into my social time, so I switched to psychology. I got my degree in that. But I've always loved photography.

When I was about twelve years old, my dad bought me a little Brownie Hawkeye camera. With it came a developing tank and a little printing deal. I would take pictures during the day, and when my dad came home at night, we would close off the bathroom for a darkroom and develop the pictures and print them.

It was magical. It has stuck with me my whole life.

After college, I got drafted into the Army and went to Vietnam. That's hard to talk about. I have a lot of sorrow and remorse for the friends I lost over there. I also walked away with some great things. I got to spend time with the great Time-Life photographer Larry Burroughs, who influenced my life greatly.

I was with the 299th Combat Engineer Battalion. Each officer was given other jobs to do besides just being an engineer. One of my jobs was public information officer, which meant that all the journalists coming into our fire base had to check with me, and I was in charge of where they went and what they did. I got to meet Peter Arnett, Sean Flynn and Larry Burroughs, some of the notable journalists.

Larry was the most incredible man I ever met. He was a brilliant man. I was in combat with him and watched him take pictures under heavy fire. When, I must say, I was scared out of my mind, he would just stand up there and take pictures. He had no fear of death. I had never met a man like that before.

I talked to him about it. He told me he felt that his mission in life was to show man's inhumanity to man. That was it. At any cost, he would do that. Eventually, Larry was killed in Cambodia.

When I got home, I wanted to follow in that man's footsteps. I wanted to be a photographer. I corresponded with his family, and I was a photojournalist for a very short period. But Larry's wife, Vicky, made a good point with me. She said, "Burt, there are things you can do with photography besides being a photojournalist. There's also art."

I decided to check out art. So I went back to North Texas and studied painting, drawing, sculpture, art history. And I was a photographer. I did some things for the Dallas Museum. I was in a group show in Houston, and I even showed with Ben Breard at the Afterimage Gallery. Ben was one of the first people to show my work. I have fond memories of that. I learned a lot from him. But I could never make a living. It's hard to make a living and do art.

For a while, I worked for my neighbor, who was in the construction business. Then I decided I would start my own construction company and did that for ten years. Commercial and residential remodeling. A lot of work for the fast-food chains and J. C. Penney. The people who worked with me were fellow artists from North Texas. It wasn't your standard construction company. We talked about art history while we worked.

It was a lot of fun. But I got involved in a lawsuit that took a lot of time and energy to settle, and I just didn't want to do that anymore. My insurance man said, "The construction people are always exposed." I didn't want that exposure anymore.

So I became a watch dealer. I've always loved vintage watches. I bought a bunch of watches from a guy and joined an organization called the National Association of Watch and Clock Collectors. It was a time when vintage watches were the hottest thing on the planet. About 1983-84.

Missy and I did that for seven years, eight years. We traveled all over the world, buying and selling watches. Mainly wristwatches. Great watches from the '20s, '30s, '40s and '50s. Pieces of art that you wear on your wrist.

In about 1986 or '87, Missy and I were in New York. I was on my way to a watch auction at Sotheby's. In one of the sales rooms they had a preview of a photography auction. I was astonished that you could actually buy those great photographs. Photographs that I had seen as slides in my history of photography courses.

The next day I went in there and bought as many photographs as I could buy with the money I had. That got me started as a collector. I would go to every auction after that.

Pretty soon I owned more photographs than I did watches. Missy and I decided that if we were going to continue buying photographs, we would have to start selling some of them. So we became private dealers and started going to shows.

One time we were going to a show in Chicago to try to sell some of what we had. But we didn't have a name or a logo or a business card. We had this rubber stamp that said "Photographs Do Not Bend" that we stamped packages with. So we bought some blank cards and stamped them with the rubber stamp and wrote our names and phone number on it, and that's what we handed out. In April 1994, when we opened up our own gallery, that's what we called the place. Photographs Do Not Bend.

I tell you, when we first started, we had a helluva lot of free time. I sat around and read and wrote people postcards. The money was not coming in. The first three years were a learning experience. We didn't know what we were doing. But it was a magical thing. Whenever we really needed help, somebody would appear at the gallery and help us out.

To me, photography is mystical. A photograph is a slice of time. It stops time. Photography lets you into a million other worlds. It's art, it's education, it's everything happening all together.

I feel good about selling photographs to people. I like the fact that they're hung in their houses and their families get to look at them and the son or daughter wonders why Dad could spend $1,500 on a piece of paper.

It seems nonsensical, doesn't it? But that's art. It's the strand that keeps the whole human race going. It's about spirit. It's almost a religion. A positive religion.

The biggest thrill I get is when a high school class comes into the gallery and I get to talk to them about photography and try to ignite a little fire in them. Like Larry Burroughs ignited in me. Like my dad ignited in me when he bought me that Brownie Hawkeye. I feel an obligation to pass that torch.

It's not about money. Ninety-five percent of the people who come in here just look. That's OK. I mean, that's what it's about.

Kenneth Adams, shoe shiner at Union Station in Dallas, is also a minister. The Bible he is holding is the one he carries with him every day. Courtesy *The Dallas Morning News*, Juan Garcia, photographer.

Kenneth Adams

Kenneth Adams, forty-eight, owns and operates
Ken's Korner, the shoeshine stand at Union
Station in downtown Dallas. He's also a minister
in the African Methodist Episcopal Church.

I was born here in Dallas on August 21, 1950. My dad was a church-going guy, and my mom was a church missionary. She was a seamstress. She made clothes. We lived in a small little house, just the three of us. I had a sister, but she moved to California. She was eighteen years old when I was born.

I had about seven stepsisters. My real mother passed when I was twelve years old, and my father married again. I found out early in life that girls always get their way with parents. The boys are last. My dad stayed at my stepmom's house, and I stayed at our old house, so I was by myself most of the time.

I was a member of the St. James AME Temple. My uncle, the Rev. C. C. Davis, was pastor of that church when I was born. He was my mother's brother. He baptized me when I was an infant. Sprinkled me. So I've been a member of the AME Church all my life. I'm a cradle AME. Now I'm a minister in the AME Church, associate pastor of Warren Chapel AME. It's a small church in West Dallas.

I graduated from Booker T. Washington High School in 1969 and went to Prairie View and El Centro College. I went to college about three years, then I dropped out. I went to leather school at the University of Texas in Tyler and took up leather design and repair. I learned all about leather. For a while I had about three trades. I was a lab technician in a biology lab, and I had a grocery store and a leather shop before I came to the shoeshine business.

I've been in the shoeshine business about seventeen years. I've been here in Union Station since November 1, 1981.

I started preaching in 1996, but I've had a ministry since 1991. I had a ministry called the Children's Program right here in Union Station. It was a once-a-year event, and I was the host. I gave clothes and toys and food baskets to children at Christmas, and I would hire clowns and everything, and we would have a Christmas party. A lot of my customers donated to it. The ladies from Amtrak, they would bake cookies.

In 1997, I caught the flu and didn't want to contaminate the children, so I donated my stuff to Santa's Helpers over there at Channel 8. Some of the people here at Union Station helped me carry it over there. We had a whole lot of toys and things. That was one of the greatest years.

I received the call to be a minister in about '92, but I was like Jeremiah. I kept running from the Lord. Then I started working a street ministry. I started hanging on the streets and talking to people and studying. I read the Bible backward and forward. The more I read, the more I started losing myself. I would find myself preaching in an empty room sometimes, singing sometimes. God was bringing me to himself.

But I was still drinking a little beer then, still straddling the fence. You have to be totally saved and believe that Jesus is the son of God before you can reap all the rewards that he has for you. When I got saved truly was when the Holy Spirit came on me. When the Holy Spirit came on me, I was happy. I didn't care about the world anymore. All doubt was gone.

God has given me all my gifts now, but they have yet to mature fully. A lot of preachers read a lot of books and go to seminary, but you put them on the street and they're shaking like a leaf. But I'm different. I've slept outdoors. I've been homeless. I've been hungry. I've been in situations where a person without the shield of God would have buckled. I've known people on these streets around here who have committed suicide.

One night I was reading the Book of Jeremiah, and the thought came to me, "He's just like me." Because Jeremiah rejected God. But God told him, "You shall go where I shall send thee, and you shall say what I command thee." In the end, Jeremiah came to be the prophet of God. That's what happened to me.

The thing I like best about my job here is my friends. Many of the people who come to me, I've known for years. We talk about all kinds of things, just like you and I are now. I meet all kinds. I've had Muslims in this chair. I've had agnostics. I've had Hindus. I've had Buddhists. I've had monks. I've had all kinds of preachers and missionaries. Some of them pray for me. Priests, prophets, Catholics. Anglicans. One man blessed this chair.

Between customers, I read my Bible and work on my sermons. I have all my sermons in this box that I keep under the chair here.

This is a great place to witness.

James Jennings is a retired Dallas policeman and was the voice of the Cotton Bowl for many years. He has visited every town on the Texas map. Courtesy *The Dallas Morning News*, John F. Rhodes, photographer.

James Jennings

James Jennings, sixty-six, has been a Dallas police officer, a Coca-Cola executive and a stadium announcer, among other occupations. Over a three-and-one-half-year period, he and his wife, Linda, visited every town in Texas. They live in Heath, Texas.

My life has been strange and different. It really has. I was born near Sulphur Springs in a manger. The doctor came out to the house to deliver me. We lived in a tiny, crude, three-room frame house about eight miles out of town.

One of the rooms was hay storage, and a window was broken out of it. The cows would come up and stick their heads through the window and eat the hay. So I tell my children I was born in a manger.

My life was constant flip-flops and struggles and working different jobs. After the Navy, I went back to the T&P Railway. I was on military leave from their auditor's office in downtown Dallas. But a desk job was not going to work any more, after the Navy. So I joined the Dallas Police Department.

I graduated from the Police Academy on April Fools' Day, 1955. I worked first in the Patrol Division in West Dallas, then later transferred to the Traffic Division and investigated accidents.

I was at the Trade Mart, waiting for President Kennedy to arrive for his speech, on the day he died. When we found out what was going on, I was sent to Parkland. I helped Lyndon Johnson's party leave the hospital. I helped load President Kennedy's casket. I helped Jackie get in the hearse with it.

Just before I left the Police Department, I was working in a school-related program that included everything from public relations to traffic safety, speaking to the youngsters, working with the civic clubs and parent groups.

By then I was also announcing high-school football games and rodeos in towns within a couple of hundred miles around Dallas. And I was doing all the announcing at the Cotton Bowl. SMU, the Cowboys. Just about every game that was played there.

I left the Police Department in '68. I was recruited away by Coca-Cola and went to work for them doing public relations in the youth market. Someone there encouraged me to run for the Dallas School Board, and I was elected three times. Then I resigned from the school board to take a promotion at Coke in management.

I stayed with Coke until 1979, when I was offered a job with Adidas in sports promotions, working with athletes in all sports. Pro teams, major colleges, Olympic-related events.

But Adidas closed their office in Dallas in '89, so I joined the Mesquite Rodeo in management. I had been an announcer there for a long time. The management job I had was eliminated when Tom Hicks and Southwest Sports bought out the rodeo and moved those types of jobs out to the Ballpark in Arlington.

But I continued to announce the rodeo. I've been announcing it since 1963. Not every week, because I also had legitimate jobs and had to travel some. But now I work it every week. I've done that for about the last ten years.

So you can see I've had a varied life.

In the early days, when I was announcing rural rodeos, I would always drive to them on the back roads, because I love the little towns. Olney and Graham and Bowie and Hillsboro and Bonham. Places like that.

One day I said to my wife, Linda, "Let's do something that has never ever been done. Let's go to every town in Texas."

We were over in Bailey County, near Muleshoe, when I said that. So we started right then and there. We visited every town in Bailey County. One of the first people we met was a real nice crop-duster. He showed us his plane and how he did his work. We watched him take off in a dirt field to go spray his cotton.

We've been in every city, town, community, village and ghost town in Texas. Not just the ones on the map, because a lot of them aren't on the official road maps. We used several guides to find them. The best one is *The Roads of Texas*. It's great. It gives you every cemetery, every cattle guard, every road of every kind.

We would use that book and attack a county at a time. We wouldn't leave that county until we had worked it all. Two hundred and fifty-four counties. A lot of the communities we went to were nothing but a sign. No businesses, maybe one or two farmhouses. But we took a picture of every sign, so we would have proof that we had been there.

We started on July 1 of '94 and finished in November of '97. After a while, we would get tired of the flatlands or the Plains, and we would go next time to the Piney Woods maybe, or the Hill Country. We jumped around. My favorite town was always the one we had just left.

I wrote down a lot of the high school mascots. The Trent Gorillas. The Progresso Red Ants. The Itasca Waumpus Cats. The Hutto Hippos. There's a statue of a hippo in downtown Hutto. The statue is bigger than the downtown.

Linda has done a count of the places we went. This is not exact, but she got around 3,300. A lot of them are not incorporated towns. There are even county seats in Texas that aren't incorporated. We've got thousands of pictures and a million memories.

We never called a chamber of commerce. We told no one we were coming. We just went into a town to see what we could see, meet who we could meet, visit with them and pick up a little information and then leave. We would be out from two days to nine days at a time. You know, it takes ten hours just to drive to the Big Bend, so you have to plan on staying a few days.

The Big Bend was our favorite region. It's absolutely great. And you've got to like the Hill Country. East Texas and its Piney Woods has its beauty. The coastline has kind of a romantic beauty.

We harvested corn north of Muleshoe and ate with the farmers about sundown on the rear of a pickup truck. We met some of the greatest people in the world. We have many, many names of folks we talked with.

A lot of people wondered who we were when we would come into a town. They knew we didn't belong there.

At Pickton, I took a picture of the domino hall from my car. Then we went to the little store to get a hamburger. One of those old domino players came over and said, "My friends over there wanted me to come and find out who you people are."

Another day we had a situation that started a little negative but turned extremely positive. I can't remember the name of the town. It was south of here. We had heard about a bank there that was over 100 years old and still had the brass teller cages. We wanted to see it.

We circled two or three times by the bank. About the fourth trip around, we stopped at a stop sign, and a heavyset man on a riding lawn mower cut us off at the intersection. He said, "Who are you people?" And I said, "Well, who are you?" And he said, "I'm the mayor of this town, and the feller on that other mower down there is the mayor pro tem. We're mowing the community center, and we saw you people. We just wondered what you was doing."

I told him what we were doing and why we were cruising by the bank. He escorted us on that lawn mower to the bank, took us in and introduced us to the president, and they let us take pictures of the brass teller cages.

Wills Point called the police on us because somebody saw us taking pictures on Main Street and the bank on the corner. They thought we were casing it.

The last county we did was Bee County, and the little town of Pawnee was the last town. I cried because I wanted to start over. Linda wanted to celebrate and have some champagne. We couldn't buy champagne in Pawnee, so we did the next best thing: We went fifteen miles out of our way to Kenedy, Texas, and split a Blizzard at the Dairy Queen.

We're doing quite a bit of speaking now on the subject. Paid appearances. Senior groups at churches, the Shriners' wives, various organizations. It's a highly popular subject. People love it.

Ed Sealy, Sr. in his hobby shop in Irving with some of his model airplanes. In his nineties, he still makes and sells balsa wood model airplane kits. Courtesy *The Dallas Morning News*, Natalie Caudill, photographer.

Ed Seay, Sr.

Ed Seay Sr. is ninety-one. He's an encyclopedia of knowledge about aircraft large and small. He and his son, Ed Jr., still run the hobby shop he opened in Irving, Texas, in 1948, where he still cuts his model airplane kits out of balsa wood.

I sold my first model, the Spirit of St. Louis, in Little Rock in 1927 for the Lindbergh tour. I had bought three kits from the Ideal Airplane Co., an early-day model airplane company in New York. It's now the Ideal Toy Co. I assembled one for myself, I sold one to a fellow, and sold the third to Pheiffer's Department Store. It was a three-foot paper-and-stick model.

Also, I sold Pheiffer's a wooden model of the Spirit of St. Louis with an eighteen-inch wingspan. They had my two models in a window there, on display. Lindbergh had just made his flight and was touring the country with his airplane. Every town he stopped in gave him a parade down Main Street, and Little Rock was one of them.

I often wonder what happened to that little wooden model. It would have lasted a lot longer than the paper-and-stick one.

I went to work at Command Air in Little Rock, an aircraft company out by the airport, on August 1 of '28. The Wall Street crash closed them up in 1929, but in a year and a half we put out more than 400 airplanes. I was building wooden ribs for them, and I was making models on the side and selling them to other employees of the company.

We were getting ready for an air show at the Coliseum in Chicago between Christmas '28 and New Year's. So the foreman of the paint shop came to me and said, "Ed, make us a model to take to the show." I made it a half-inch-to-the-foot model, sixteen-inch wingspan, of the Command Air. The paint shop foreman was painting the parts of it for me before I assembled it. While he was doing this, the head of the company came through, showing a customer the plant and saw the foreman painting the model. The foreman said, "Oh, we make little ones, too."

The head of the company borrowed that model and hung it up in his office. He never did pay me anything for it. When Wall Street crashed, I got it back. I still have it.

In the spring of '29, 185 people were working at Command Air, and we were putting out two airplanes a day. Fabric-covered wood wings, steel-tube fuselage, places for three people. Sometimes, with the assembly crew working on Sunday, we got out fourteen planes that week instead of twelve.

When I went to work at Chance-Vought Experimental in Dallas in '48, it took 17,000 people to put out one F8 Crusader a day. The state of the art had increased that much.

After the crash hit, I went back home to Arkadelphia. My mother and I and my sister were in the nursery and florist business there. I set up a workbench in the attic of the greenhouse office and started building models up there.

Our parts man at Command Air, W. F. Scott Jr.—we called him Scotty—had become the supply division parts man for Curtiss-Wright in East St. Louis, Illinois. He was an old bachelor and set him up bachelor quarters in a basement at the plant, right there on the airport. He was a good friend of Dr. Seuss, and Dr. Seuss painted up his walls and shower stall and everything. It was something to see. I'd love to have pictures of that.

Anyway, whenever Scotty would go out to take orders for airplane parts, he would also take orders for my models. And I paid him his commission in models.

In '32, I rode my new Indian motorcycle—a $355 Scout 45—all the way to Detroit in the snow, sleet, and rain to attend the National Aircraft Show. I didn't know what business cards were. I had a little model airplane I had made—three-inch wingspan—

that I carried around in my pocket. I knew the specs on all the civilian and military airplanes made in the United States at that time. And I would get people's attention showing them my little model and pass out order blanks to them instead of business cards.

In ten days I took 442 orders for model airplanes. It took me to the summer of '33 to build them all, with my sister helping me paint them. Plus the orders coming in from Scotty. I was selling them for $1.50 to $15 each.

Anyway, I came to Texas and worked for a model airplane company, Golden Aircraft Corp., from February '35 to December '35. Captain Jack Davis owned the company. He was in business from '34 to '37.

Then I went out to Love Field and lived in a dormitory with the other single employees and went to work for Dallas Aviation School. I lived in the dormitory for three years and then got a room with a family, which is where I met my wife, Mildred. She was a Taylor. They were out of East Texas. Over 150 used to show up at their family reunions.

I didn't drink or smoke, and Mildred and I had a good marriage. I lost her a little over six years ago. We were just starting our 56th year together.

I taught the first class of Air Corps cadets to hit Love Field. I taught them aerodynamics and the theory of flight and aircraft maintenance. There were sixty-nine in the first class. Five were master's degrees and the rest of them had college degrees. That was the bunch I was trying to teach. There was one West Pointer sent down to be the commandant and drill the boys.

I washed out thirteen of those boys because they couldn't get the theory of flight and aerodynamics. That was the statistic they had predicted—that thirteen out of the sixty-nine would wash out. And the same thirteen I washed out had washed out of everything else, too. So it was a pretty good statistic, wasn't it?

Thing was, General Hap Arnold had come back from the Battle of Britain in late '39 and called the operators of the twelve major aviation schools in the country to St. Louis and said, "Boys, we've got to start training pilots. We can't wait for Congress to act." He said, "I'll furnish you cadets and give you some old airplanes, and it'll be up to you to house and feed these boys."

Major Bill Long, who owned the Dallas Aviation School, made himself a millionaire several times over on eight or ten military contracts. He had cadets training at Love Field, Terrell, Midland, Big Spring. He had been a pilot in the observation squadron that went to France in World War I and came back and established the Dallas Aviation School in the '20s.

I found out that the second class of cadets at Love Field was going to be sixty-nine West Pointers, and I didn't want anything to do with them snobs. Lieutenant Estes, the commandant, was a pretty nice guy to be a West Pointer. Unusual.

The old airplanes that Arnold gave us were PT3s, made by Consolidated, with a Whirlwind J5 in the front of them. And we hired all the instructors we could get. At the end of five or six months, we got P17s to replace the PT3s.

I was an instructor there seven and a half years, from December of '35 until June of '43. There never was an accident coming out of my shop, working student labor. The CAA [Civil Aeronautics Administration] came to me and said, "How would you like to work for us?" And I stepped into a government job and moved up to Stillwater, Oklahoma, to keep an eye on the bases there and at Ponca City and Alva. A green 1944 coupe was furnished with the job.

I stayed with the CAA for a year and a half, then they loaned me to the Defense Plant Corporporaton to store surplus airplanes. I was the government man who received them from the ferry pilots and assigned them over to storage contractors. I put over 800 in Muskogee at Hatbox Field.

The last week of January 1945, I went to work for Lockheed at their modification center at Love Field and was building models on the side. I put out a little balsa wood glider, and I made a little rubber-powered propeller airplane. I made over 60,000 of them before I lost the source of my pre-cut balsa propellers. Now I've found a box of the old props and I'm putting out that old airplane as an antique.

I get $4.50 for the little glider now. I used to sell it for twenty-five cents. I haven't put a price on the antique yet. I'm thinking about ten bucks.

I moved into this hobby shop in January of '48 and built me an apartment in the back. I called it the M-A-L Hobby Shop. That stands for Model Aircraft Labs.

The following March, I sold my house in Dallas and moved out here. My wife got mad at me for selling the house. But I was in the hole, bankrupt, but I wouldn't take bankruptcy. I moved out here and pulled myself up again. We lived here for a number of years and finally bought the property.

This was an open field out here for four years. I must have taught two or three dozen kids to fly on that field. Then they built the movie theater across the street, and there was a skating rink at the corner where Atlas Plumbing is now.

I worked at Chance-Vought Experimental for ten years, from '48 to '59. I helped build the first F8 Crusaders. I was a mechanic. My wife worked behind the counter here at the shop.

The big aircraft companies would hire me to make a model of each plane they built, and they would give it to the customer when they delivered the plane. And I was a model judge over at the State Fair for a number of years, until my son took over for me.

The last twelve years, I've been with three or four big law firms in Dallas, making models of air-related collisions. They use my models to simulate the accident at the trials. I make $350 per model. The first case I was on, I had to look at over 400 color slides to determine how the model should be painted.

I've been in business on this spot for fifty-two years. I built my reputation on my saw-cut balsa wood kits. My best saw that I've ever gotten hold of was a Black & Decker hollow-ground combination blade. After sixty years using my saws, I still have all my fingers.

There's only about four of us left, cutting this extra-light wood for the builders of indoor model airplanes. I cut the wood and make up these kits and sell them for $10 to $55. My son and I go to about a dozen model airplane meets, conventions and shows every year, all over the country. I just got back from one in Pensacola. I drove down there in two days, spent two days there, then drove back. No trouble.

It pays to go. In four hours at Pensacola, I did over $600 in business.

Oksana Marchenko is a young artist who immigrated to Dallas from the former Soviet Union. She poses in her home in front of a mural which she recently finished. Courtesy *The Dallas Morning News*, Ariane Kadoch, photographer.

Oksana Marchenko

Oksana Marchenko, thirty-three, is a mural artist and portrait painter. She emigrated from Russia to the United States with her husband and young daughter in the 1990s. They now live in Plano.

Ten days ago I became a citizen of the United States. My daughter became a citizen when I did. And this morning at eight o'clock my husband did. It's a good feeling. We weren't citizens of anywhere. It was because of what happened to the Soviet Union, and because we lived in Latvia before we moved here.

I was born in Russia, in the far east, near Vladivostok. I used to be an acrobat. When I was eight years old, I dedicated my life to the circus. I trained for about nine years in the children's circus, and then I went to try to get into circus college in Moscow. It was impossible. I went back home, I finished high school and went back to Moscow to try again. I didn't get in that time, either.

I went back home and worked at the machine factory. At that time it was a military factory. I worked there for a couple of months, then I went back to Moscow to try again to get into the circus. I found out I didn't need a diploma from the circus college. I went to see a *narogny* artist, a person who had gotten a people's award for excellence. She tested my acrobatic skills. She told me, "Good!" and I got into the Moscow Circus.

I was one of five girls who did beautiful acrobatic dancing on a pedestal, a white table. Artistic acrobatics. Every one of us had a different color costume. Mine was blue, and I had a blue light on me. My partner had a red costume and a red light on her. The five of us were like an artist's palette, a beautiful, dancing palette.

Besides working as an acrobat, I started acting a little. We did children's fairy tales in the circus during Christmastime, that sort of thing. I also worked with the Russian bears, even though I didn't want to. They're dangerous. They're unpredictable animals. But the gentleman I worked with, he needed a partner. So I worked with the bears also.

For five years I worked with the circus. Then in 1986 I got married. I met my husband, Evgeny, in Riga, Latvia, which was part of the Soviet Union at the time. I worked for another year, and then in 1988 our daughter, Sabrina, was born and I left the circus.

Evgeny is a professional athlete, a five-time world champion in acrobatics. When I met him, he was on the Soviet team. Originally he's from Kazakhstan, but he moved to Latvia when he became a professional athlete. He lived there for about ten years.

In order for us to get an apartment, he had to serve in the Soviet army. He did it for a couple of years, competing in acrobatics so the army would get some credit for his performances. That way we could have an apartment and he could train eight hours a day.

When Latvia became independent in 1991, they kicked out every Soviet military person. We were hoping to get our citizenship in Latvia. Evgeny thought he had to do something for Latvia, so he decided to compete for Latvia as an independent country. In 1991 he went to Portugal to compete in the European championships. He won a gold medal. It was the first gold medal for an independent Latvia in fifty-four or fifty-six years.

But for Russians in Latvia, life is very difficult. Evgeny was a champion for Latvia, but he was Russian, and the Latvians didn't care about his gold medal. They wouldn't give him citizenship. Our daughter didn't have citizenship. We used to have a Russian citizenship, but because we lived in Latvia it all kind of melted away, disappeared.

There was no future for our daughter in Latvia. We had to leave. Evgeny was invited to many countries to work as a coach. Australia, Belgium, France, just anywhere he would choose to go.

But the United States was for us. There are a lot of opportunities here for anybody. Anybody who is a hard worker, of course. Europe is so small. Everything is already occupied. There is no space. Everything is already processed and produced and invented in Europe. Australia is too far.

Evgeny and his partner, Natasha Regkova, were invited to perform in New Orleans. After the show, Evgeny got an offer to work at one of the gymnastics clubs there. He accepted and worked in New Orleans for a year and a half.

We liked New Orleans, but people there have a different view of gymnastics. Gymnastics is a tough sport. You have to work hard. And New Orleans is a touristy place. They like to party and have fun. Mardi Gras. Nobody works at Mardi Gras. We thought we should go somewhere else. When we received our green cards, we decided to go about our own business.

Now Evgeny has a school here in Plano, the World Olympic Gymnastics Academy. He has a partner, Valerie Liukin. Valerie was an Olympic gymnastics champion in 1988. He's from Kazakhstan. He also competed for the Soviet Union, like Evgeny. His wife, Anna Liukin, is a world champion in gymnastics.

Evgeny and Valerie did the research about where we should go. They looked for the best public schools and the most family-oriented place they could find. Valerie and Evgeny thought Plano was the best choice. They are partners in the academy, and Anna Liukin and Natasha Regkova teach there. We've all been here for seven years now.

Dallas is very different from New Orleans. Dallas is a workaholic kind of place. Everybody works hard. We like that about it.

I didn't speak any English when I arrived, but what I saw on people's faces from the first day I arrived was smiles. That made the strongest impression on me. And freedom of action. Everywhere, everywhere, at the store, at the movie theater, people are doing what they want to. Freedom. People don't limit themselves.

But people here are quiet. At the store, nobody is screaming, nobody is yelling. In Russia it's different, maybe because of the poverty. Children in Russia, when they see something beautiful, something they want, they cry. My mom noticed this when she came to visit me. She said, "Children don't cry here. Why is that?"

Freedom. That's what made me decide that, yes, I can try my skills in different fields. I worked at a financial firm for a while as an office manager. I did some research in the telecommunications field. I did a variety of jobs, even without a special education. In Russia you can't do this.

For women in Russia, professions are very limited. If you are not at an age before twenty-five years old, you can't really get a profession. There are certain qualities you have to have. You have to have long legs and you have to be beautiful. To get a career going in Moscow or St. Petersburg, you have to be not just educated and highly intelligent. You also have to have the legs. But here you don't really have to have any of this. You just have to work hard and you can get wherever you want to be.

When my husband decided to come here, that's what he felt about this country. The possibilities are endless. In Russia people can be highly intelligent, and most people are, and they can have the highest education, but after a young person graduates from a top university, there aren't many possibilities, not many opportunities to grow in his field.

Like my sister. She's educated. She has two diplomas, in chemistry and economics. She was supposed to work at the paper factory. She's beautiful. She even has the long legs. But she can't find a job. In the area of Russia where she lives, the economy is pretty much shut down.

I would like to bring her here, which I'm working on right now. I would like for her to get an education here in one of the cosmetology centers.

I've always loved painting. I've painted all my life, since I was a child. It was always either the circus or painting. I could never choose, so I did both. When I had to make a choice about my profession, I chose the circus. But while working with the circus, I always did some painting. It didn't disappear. It's in my blood.

After I came here I worked for two years in the fashion modeling business. Not because that was my goal. I was trying to figure out what I could do in this country. And a photographer, Roger Moore, and I did some print work for a cosmetics company. Roger and I became friends. Because of him I met Kay Harris. She's a well-known interior designer in Dallas. I started working with her.

She let me paint murals. For some reason, she trusted me with those big walls. And I was brave enough to touch those expensive walls in those expensive homes in Highland Park and University Park. That's how I gained my confidence. I love my walls. I love my brush. Paint is my friend. I haven't forgotten anything.

I started learning more. I took some classes at Collin County Community College. Then I decided, I can do it! I can do it! I gained more confidence. I paint murals, I paint frescoes, I like painting furniture, I do portraits. I don't limit myself. I like working with different media. I like to experiment.

Now I know for sure that this is what I really want, this is what I'm supposed to be doing in this life.

Sabrina, our daughter, is eleven now. She's bilingual. She speaks Russian, she reads Russian. I try my best to help her keep her originality, her Russian-ness, because it's given by God, and there's no way I'm going to let it disappear.

It's good to have more than one language. Sabrina studies Spanish in school, and on her own she studies French. The United States is becoming more and more a multilingual country. That's wonderful. It's good for America. And we're American now.

Beatrice Woolley, mother of *The Dallas Morning News* writer Bryan Woolley.
Courtesy *The Dallas Morning News*, Andy Scott, photographer.

Beatrice Woolley

Beatrice Woolley is my mother. She lives in Dallas now. This piece was published as a Mother's Day tribute.

I grew up on a farm in Hamilton County near a little town named Carlton. My daddy, Audie Gibson, was a farmer and then became a peace officer, a deputy sheriff. My mother, Clora Gibson, was a teacher. I was an only child.

Carlton was just a little sleepy farm town. It was country people. Good people. Everybody knew everybody and everybody's business. Carlton was where my daddy was killed.

It was a snowy night just before Christmas, in 1932. In those days there was no antifreeze for cars, so you had to drain your radiator at night in cold weather to keep it from freezing up.

Daddy got a phone message that night from the man who owned the drugstore and lived behind it. He said some men were trying to rob his store. Daddy decided to walk down there, rather than put water in the radiator and drive.

It wasn't far. Just down a hill. When he got about halfway to the store, two men attacked him. They shot him with his own gun.

Another man was sitting in a car, waiting for them. The two men ran toward the car, but they found out that a group had formed a posse and were after them, so they took off on foot.

They were found in a field out from town a little way. The man who found them, Jim Pierce, was unarmed. But he made a fist in his coat pocket and pushed it into one of the fellows' back. The fellows thought it was a gun. Jim caught them that way. And they caught the fellow in the car and called the sheriff. He came over from Hamilton and took them to jail. They went to prison for life.

I was sixteen when it happened. Mother and I stayed in our home for a while, and then we moved into an apartment. I think Mother sold the house. The apartment was very small. A bedroom, kitchenette and bath. It was at Uncle Ben and Aunt Ann Smith's house in Carlton.

I graduated from high school the next May. School ended in March or April because it was the Depression. The school year was shortened because the trustees couldn't afford to pay the teachers. The seniors had to take a test. Those who passed graduated, those who didn't had to go another year. I graduated as salutatorian and went to John Tarleton College in Stephenville the next fall. The last gift my daddy gave me was my class ring.

Tarleton was a junior college then. I don't know how we got the money for me to go. College didn't cost so much then, of course, but Mother made a small salary.

I lived in the dormitory and waited tables there the first year. I was not good at it. They wanted you to carry the tray way up high, above your shoulder, and I couldn't do that. After that, I had to move out of the dormitory. I couldn't afford it.

Six of us moved out and roomed with a widow lady with two grown children. We enjoyed that. We liked it much better than the dormitory. It was much cheaper, and we were all poor girls. One of the girls had been a beauty operator. She did our hair every Saturday. We had a real good life there. I finished the two years of Tarleton and graduated, but I couldn't afford to go on. I guess that was one of the reasons I got married.

My husband and I went to Waco on our honeymoon. Waco is only about eighty miles from Carlton, but I had never been there. Then we went to the Texas Centennial in Dallas. We took in all the sights, but I don't remember much about it.

I guess you could say my husband farmed for a living. We had five kids, close together. Three boys and two girls. None of them were born two years apart. Two were just thirteen months apart.

During the war my husband had to go into the service. He was drafted. He thought I had something to do with it, but I didn't. I don't know why he thought that. He was injured in basic training. He never went overseas.

When he came back, he was different. He didn't do much of anything in the way of work. He wouldn't support the family. He started running around with a neighbor woman. I couldn't take it. I moved the kids to town, to my mother's house. My husband's family sold the farm.

I was so upset and tired. Mother and I called my uncles in Marfa, Texas. My mother's brothers. They wanted us to come out there for a visit. So we drove Mother's 1939 Chevrolet from Carlton to Marfa with the five kids. All the highways were two-lane then. It was a long trip.

We stayed about ten days. My Uncle Emmitt DeVolin was friends with the superintendent of schools in Fort Davis, Mr. C. G. Matthews, and he knew there were some vacancies for teachers over there. So he made an appointment for Mother to see Mr. Matthews.

Mother and I and the three youngest kids went over to Fort Davis, and Mother got the school, teaching third and fourth grades. That same day, we rented a little apartment without the landlady knowing we had two more kids. She was surprised later when the whole family showed up.

So we moved to Fort Davis. And there we stayed.

I took in sewing and substituted at the school some. I became friends with the county judge's wife, Betty Granger, who owned a little dry goods store. She sold me sewing supplies. The judge knew the man who was county clerk was going to retire and go to his ranch, and he wanted me to run for the office. I told him I couldn't even type, which was a big part of the job. He said, "That's all right. You can learn."

So I did it. And he and his wife helped me electioneer. I had cards printed, asking people to vote for me. Jeff Davis is a big county and there were only about 500 voters and they were scattered out. We went from house to house and to the ranches and over to Valentine, and I handed out the cards and told people who I was. Sometimes I had some of the kids on the back seat of the car.

And I got the job. I was the first woman ever elected to that office. The Mexican-American people were almost 100 percent for me, because they knew what it was like to have children and have a hard time making a living. I was elected without any trouble at all. This was 1946. The Democratic primary was in July then.

So we went back to Carlton to sell Mother's house and get what furniture we wanted to keep. My daddy's brother had a truck, and he and his wife hauled our things out to Fort Davis for us. They thought they were driving to the end of the earth.

I had a friend in Carlton who had taught typing at the high school, and while we were there she taught me the keyboard. Then Bill Granger, the judge, brought me a typewriter from the courthouse, and I just practiced, practiced, practiced. By the time I took office in January, I could type.

Moving to Fort Davis was the greatest thing that ever happened to me. It completely changed our life. We didn't have any life in Carlton. There wouldn't have been any. In Carlton, getting a divorce back then was almost shameful. Only people who were not much got divorces. Of course, everybody knew my circumstances. I had to get out of there.

My husband filed for divorce against me. I filed a counter suit. The judge heard our case in his chambers. When my lawyer showed a picture of me and my children to the judge, my husband's lawyer said, "I don't have a case," and walked out of the room. My husband looked very surprised.

I was supposed to get $50 a month child support. But he never paid unless I called the sheriff or the judge where he was living, and they would make him send a check. But he would never voluntarily send it. He only sent two or three checks.

One day the Jeff Davis County commissioners court was discussing our salaries. One of the commissioners, Mr. Herbert

Kokernot, bless his heart, turned to me and said, "Mrs. Woolley, would a $50-a-month raise help you?" I said, "Oh, yes!" I never tried again to get child support, and my husband never sent any more. The Lord took care of it.

Fort Davis was a little mountain town. A ranchers' town. Everybody knew everybody, and everybody was interested in our family. And my mother was such a good teacher. Everybody liked her. She was prominent in the town.

We bought a big adobe house from an old bachelor, George Grierson. We paid $7,500, I think it was. It was big enough to take care of everybody, and we made a home out of it. It was headquarters for all the neighborhood kids. They came in and out all the time.

Fort Davis was a great place to raise children. The parents watched out for each other's kids. The sheriff, Wilbur Medley, was a friend of mine because we worked together, and he knew what all the kids were doing. But he didn't tell me anything unless he thought I needed to know it. None of my kids ever got in any serious trouble. Sometimes they had to be straightened out, but it was for nothing bad.

It wasn't easy for two women not making much money to raise that many children. But God just took care of us. We made it. Those were good days. We had a lot of love. Every one of the five went to college and got their degrees. Some of them got more than one.

I had only two opponents run against me the whole time I was in office. Both were older women. When I started, we had only two-year terms instead of four. I hadn't been in office a year before this woman came to me and told me she had to have a job, so she was going to run against me.

She was an old-timer in Fort Davis, but nobody liked her. Even her husband's family didn't like her. Her husband had been the sheriff, and he was shot about two years after my daddy was.

I told her I had to have a job, too, and I beat her. Her relatives didn't even vote for her. A few years later, a woman who had retired from McDonald Observatory ran against me. She didn't get anywhere. She left town right after the election. Moved away.

Nobody tried after that. I was county and district clerk for thirty-three years. I resigned before my last term was out. I had bought the Jeff Davis County Abstract Co., and I wanted to get my business going.

I have thirteen grandchildren, and the great-grandchildren just keep coming. I'm going to have to count them again. For an only child, I have quite a few descendants. And all of them are fine.

Dale Long

Dale Long, Community Outreach Coordinator for the City of Dallas, was in the 16th Street Baptist Church in Birmingham, Alabama, on September 15, 1963, when it was bombed and four girls were killed. Top to bottom, at right, Denise McNair, Carol Robertson, Cynthia Wesley, and Addie Mae Collins. Courtesy *The Dallas Morning News*, Cheryl Diaz Meyer, photographer.

Dale Long

On September 15, 1963, a bomb explosion tore through the basement of the 16th Street Baptist Church in Birmingham, Alabama, killing four young girls. Two men, including one living in Mabank, Texas, have only recently been convicted of the murders. Two of the suspects have died. Dale Long, then eleven years old, was in the church when the bomb exploded. He's now a community outreach coordinator for the city of Dallas and a civic leader in Garland, where he lives with his wife and two daughters.

I was born in 1952. I grew up in Birmingham. I went to grade school and high school there. My maternal grandparents were big members of the 16th Street Baptist Church. It's a huge church, one of the oldest in Birmingham. As a child growing up, that's all I knew.

Church was every Sunday. My mother and her sister grew up in that church, and my brother and I did, also. We participated in youth activities. The Easter plays, the Christmas plays. We played in the church orchestra. In the summer we did Bible School.

The church is situated on the edge of downtown Birmingham, right across the street from Kelly Ingram Park, which in the '60s was the nucleus of the civil rights demonstrations. That's the park where Bull Connor used the fire hoses and the dogs.

The bombing of the church was the most devastating thing that ever happened, even though growing up with the Jim Crow laws was pretty frustrating. You can't do this. You can't do that. Because you're black.

I recall begging my dad to take us to see *The Shaggy Dog*. We went to the Melba Theater in downtown Birmingham. It was during the wintertime, so it was dark. We entered from the alley. My dad was dressed in his Sunday suit. I remember walking up some dark outdoor steps to the balcony, which is where black folk had to sit. There were no lights. We had to feel our way up. They were so filthy I remember my feet sticking to the steps.

I went to see that movie when I was seven or eight years old. That experience taught me why my folks didn't want to take us to the theater. I was too young to understand why things were like that, but I understood why my dad didn't want to do this. He never did it again. From time to time, we would go to one of the black theaters, but the features that they played were years old.

My parents watched my younger brother and me pretty closely, especially me, because I had issues with the quality of life we had. Martin Luther King's nephews went to school with us. I was hearing about the movement from them. Their daddy was a minister, so he was self-employed, so to speak. If they got arrested, they would trace the kids back to the church and nothing would happen to them.

But if I was arrested and they traced me back to my mom, it was very likely that she would lose her job. She was a schoolteacher. My dad worked two jobs. He worked for the federal Department of Labor. He also worked in the office of a motel there in Birmingham.

My parents were struggling to pay for our house and cars. Even though they were extremely sympathetic to what was going on, and in the movement in heart and spirit, it would have been devastating for one of them to lose their jobs. So we didn't participate in the demonstrations for fear of being arrested and it having an economic effect on the family.

The morning of the bombing was an average morning in September. Everybody was excited about school. It was football season. It was Youth Day at the church, which meant that the kids would take over the service. We would read the scripture, say the prayers, take the collection and so forth.

The church had been threatened several times because it had opened its doors to the Southern Christian Leadership Conference and allowed them to use its facilities for their mass rallies. There was a lot of discussion among the deacons and the trustees as to what the consequences might be. The Klan and others like them had told black folk in Birmingham what we could expect them to do.

Arthur Shores, for example, they blew up his house three or four times. Every time he would build it back, they would blow it up again. He was an attorney, an outstanding, bold leader in the movement.

When the Armstrong boys integrated the white school a block from us, the FBI came to my parents and warned them to keep an eye on their kids, because we looked a lot like the Armstrong boys.

My mother normally would have gone to Sunday school with us, but she had some kind of big school project due the next day and decided to stay home and work on it. She dropped me and my brother off at the church. He went to his Sunday school class and I went to mine.

Mr. William Greer, a high school principal, was my Sunday schoolteacher. I never will forget. He was talking to us about it being a brand new school year and us having a great opportunity to do good. My class met in the church library, about four doors down from where the bomb went off.

After class, the members of the church orchestra always got their instruments and music together before going upstairs to the church service. But for some reason, we boys stayed in the library after Sunday school that day. We were looking through the books and talking amongst ourselves.

The girls were putting on their choir robes when they died. Four were killed. I remember a solitary light bulb hanging from a cord. I remember the light disintegrating. The building shook. We heard later that there were two explosions, but I don't remember hearing them. There was dust and smoke like I had never experienced before. The lights were out.

I remember us boys looking at each other in amazement, and then just taking off running. I grew up in that church. I knew it like the back of my hand. Even though the lights were off, I knew where I was. There was a ray of sunlight coming from the stairwell. I followed that light up the steps. I think I was the first person to exit the church.

The police met me at the door. Less than a minute after the explosion, they met me on the stairs. A policeman tried to cover the entire stairwell, but I ran under his arm. He was saying, "Get back down there, nigger." But I kept going. Once I got out and realized it was a bomb, I wondered how the police had got there so fast. They were already roping off the street. It was clear that they knew in advance that it was going to happen.

There was an eerie quiet outside. Pigeons were flying all over the place. I could smell the dynamite. I couldn't believe that this had happened to a church. Of course, churches had been bombed before. But my grandmother had always taught us, if anything happens, go to the church. It's a sanctuary. I couldn't believe that people who worship the same God and read the same Bible would stoop so low.

I went back into the building to find my brother. Nobody was in his classroom. Firemen and some men of the church were down in the basement looking for folk. I could see their silhouettes. But my brother wasn't there. I found him outside with his Sunday schoolteacher and five or six other kids. Everybody was in tears.

In a few minutes, I saw my dad running down the street. My dad never ran anywhere, but he was running that day. He had a look on his face that I'll never forget. He was scared to death. He hugged us. We were crying. He kept asking us, over and over again, "Are you all right?"

On one of the black radio stations, we heard about the deaths. But they didn't say who died. Later in the afternoon, they announced the names of the girls who were killed. We were all in shock, because we knew the girls. Cynthia Wesley, Addie Mae Collins, Carole Robertson, Denise McNair. We knew them.

Retired Dallas County Sheriff's Deputy Terry Baker researches officers who have been killed in the line of duty, and thus is able to get their names installed on memorials in Austin and Washington. Courtesy *The Dallas Morning News*, Lawrence Jenkins, photographer.

Terry Baker

Terry Baker, sixty-two, served as a deputy in the Dallas County Sheriff's Department for many years. He retired as assistant chief deputy at the end of 1994. He and his wife Joyce live in Dallas.

One day a couple of years before I retired from the Sheriff's Department, a young lady came forward who said she thought a grandfather of hers was a deputy who had been killed in the line of duty.

We weren't aware of him. No one in the department knew anything about it. So they gave the information to me to check out. I was the deputy chief at the time. I looked into it and found that, yes, the young lady's grandfather had been a deputy. His name was Willis Glover Champion, and he had been killed in the line of duty while preventing an escape in the old jail in 1923.

While I was doing that research, I learned that Sidney Welk, the person who killed deputy Champion, had also killed another of our deputies, Thomas Woods, during a whiskey raid out in the river bottoms between Rowlett and Garland.

I did the research, prepared the material and got those two officers submitted to the National Law Enforcement Officers Memorial in Washington, D.C., and the new Texas Peace Officers Memorial in Austin on the grounds of the capital. The Sheriffs Association of Texas also has a memorial called the Lost Lawman Memorial. It's in Austin, and it's for sheriffs, deputies, and jailers. All the memorials are for officers who were killed in the line of duty.

About two and a half years after I retired, two young men came to the sheriff's office, and they thought they had a great-great-uncle who had been killed in the 1890s. They thought he was a deputy sheriff. So the sheriff had someone call me and, being as I'm still a certified officer and had worked those other two cases, they asked me to do the research.

So I did. His name was Addison C. Pate. I spent days and days of research at the downtown library. Finally, I came across a newspaper article from September 9, 1895. The headline said, "Pate Killed in Line of Duty." Two robbery suspects killed him at the Commerce Street wagon bridge that went across the Trinity River. There had been a robbery at Eagle Ford, which was way out in West Dallas.

When I verified that case, I thought, "Now this is three Dallas deputies killed in the line of duty that we didn't know about. There's bound to be more."

So I started looking and found another one, Charles H. Nichols, who was killed in 1871 by John Younger, a brother of the outlaws Cole and Jim Younger. A friend of Nichols' who was with him was also killed. He had been deputized by deputy Nichols, so he also was eligible for the memorials.

After that, I just started going through the old files and the newspaper microfilm, and I found other officers around the state who had been killed in the line of duty. So I would call the memorials to see if their names were there. A lot of them were not.

The list of names that I had started building was expanding. A lot of the officers were from small towns and small counties. But I also found two Fort Worth police officers who were killed in 1909 and 1915, and nobody knew about them.

I've gone as far as Duval County and La Salle County to the south to research cases. I just got back from El Paso. We researched seven officers out in the Big Bend country.

I'm working on a marshal who was killed in Pecos, Ty Morehead. He was killed February 8, 1914. The man who killed him worked as a gravedigger. When they arrested him the next day, he was digging Mr. Morehead's grave. Isn't that weird?

I'm working on two sheriffs in Presidio County, Blackie Morrow and Ernest Hamilton. And I have the name of one in Jeff Davis County, Lee Sproul.

When I go on the road, Joyce helps me with the research. We find the information that's out there in the courthouses, the funeral homes, and the cemeteries.

As of right now, I have verified fifty-six officers who were not in the memorials and sent in their files. I have another ten cases completed. The research is done. The writing-up I have to do is a lot of work, and copying the material, putting the files together.

I give copies of each file to the head of whatever agency the dead officer worked for. Also, the local library and the local historical museum, if there is one. And I give a copy to the relatives. Of course I send copies to the three memorials, and I give the Dallas County Sheriff's Department a copy, and I keep a copy.

Once I started getting known for doing this, people started calling me. And the officials at the memorials in Washington, D.C., and Austin have referred cases to me.

The two years that I've been doing this, I've been doing twenty-four or twenty-five cases a year. I work on sheriffs, deputy sheriffs, city police officers and chiefs of police, city marshals, constables and deputy constables. I haven't worked on Texas Rangers because I think they're doing their research at the Texas Ranger Hall of Fame in Waco.

Each case takes an average of about two months. Some I can do quickly. Others take a long time. I worked on one for four months and never got enough information to complete it.

I've had families write me cards and call me after I've sent them the file about an officer who was a relative. Some of them are very emotional.

One woman in Mesquite was shocked when I gave her the file on her grandmother, Kassie Mae Chandler, who had been a Dallas County matron and had been killed in 1948 in the jail. She has just been recognized as the first female officer killed in the line of duty in Texas. Her granddaughter couldn't believe it. She was absolutely amazed.

So this is what I do. The names just come out of the woodwork. No telling how many Texas officers have been killed in the line of duty. I don't want them to be forgotten. I have no trouble finding cases to work on.

Gwendolyn Leakey, a singer on local radio and television, with a picture of herself and Elvis Presley taken when they toured Texas together. Courtesy *The Dallas Morning News*, Milton Hinnant, photographer.

Gwendolyn Leakey

From the 1940s to the 1980s, Gwendolyn Wilkinson
was a singer and yodeler performing in Fort Worth,
Dallas, Hollywood, and Las Vegas under the names
Shirley Davis and Sherry Davis. She now lives in
Dallas with her husband, Hal Leakey.

My name originally was Gwendolyn Joy Wilkinson. I grew up in Fort Worth, but I was back and forth between Fort Worth and Dallas when I was a kid because I was in so many singing contests. At movie theaters between features, they used to have contests. By getting all us kids up there to sing or dance, they drew people into the theater. The kids' parents or grandparents, you know.

My first job as a professional singer was at WBAP radio in Fort Worth with the Texo Hired Hands from the Burrus Mills. The same guys were also the Light Crust Doughboys. At least some of them were.

In late '49 or '50, they opened the first television station in Fort Worth and decided they had nothing to show. So they did a program on Friday night called The Bewley Barn Dance. I sang on that, too. Bewley Mills and Burrus Mills were competitors. They both made flour.

Burrus had given me the name Shirley Davis because they didn't like Gwendolyn Wilkinson for country music. Then Bewley turned around and made it Sherry Davis because they were in competition with Burrus and didn't want the public to know I was the same girl. How anyone could mistake my yodeling, I don't know. But anyway . . .

There was a kid there named Darrell Glenn, our male vocalist. And his dad, Artie Glenn, wrote a song called "Crying in the

Chapel," and he wanted Darrell to record it. So we all went over to their house and did it on a home recorder. They sent it to all the major record companies and nothing happened. Finally, a small record label picked it up and it sold about 500,000 copies. So Darrell left to go on tour, and we needed a new male vocalist.

I was in the control room at the radio station when they were auditioning this guy, and they asked me, "How do you like him?" I said, "He's good-looking, but I don't like his voice." And they said, "Well, I'm sorry, but we're going to have to hire him whether you like him or not." I said, "Why?" And they said, "He's Red Foley's son-in-law. His name's Pat Boone."

Maybe he had some vocal training after that, but I didn't think his voice at that time had the quality that we needed. Anyway, he stayed with us until he got his first hit record, which was "Two Hearts, Two Kisses Make One Love."

Not long after that, I moved to California and went to work on television out there on *The Foreman Phillips Show*. We did five shows a week and a three-hour show on Sundays.

I worked with a man there named Merle Travis, who wrote "Sixteen Tons." We always closed the show with a gospel song, and Tennessee Ernie Ford, who had been a DJ out there on radio, would always come in to sing bass on the gospel.

One afternoon he got there early, and he and Merle were talking together about "Sixteen Tons," which Merle thought was a great song, but his record of it wasn't selling. Then Ernie said, "Why don't you do this?" and he started snapping his fingers. Then he started singing the song, and Merle just flipped out. They cut it again with Ernie singing it, and that's how he got his start.

In 1955, when I was twenty-two, my mother died, and they decided to bury her back here. She had been my chaperon. She went everywhere with me. I had three months when I didn't want to sing or anything. I stayed with my aunt and uncle in Fort Worth. Then I came to Oak Cliff and stayed with my daddy's sister and her husband. I called them Mammy and Pappy.

One day Pappy came home and told me they were auditioning girl singers for a Thursday night show on KRLD sponsored by Morris Robinson Dodge. So I went and did the audition. They didn't let me come home. I stayed there and did the show that night. Later I worked at WFAA again. I worked on KLIF, doing radio commercials. I did the Big D Jamboree at the Sportatorium on Saturday nights.

All the big stars were on the Big D Jamboree. Johnny Cash. Carl Perkins. Cowboy Copas. Elvis was on there, but I didn't see him perform there. I never met many of the stars, in fact. While the show was on, I was always up in Mr. Mac's office—Mr. Ed McLemore that owned the Sportatorium—studying my Sunday school lesson. I would stay in the office until it was time to go down and do my few songs, then I would go home and get ready for Sunday school the next morning.

I was sitting here last night scribbling a list of some of the people with whom and for whom I've worked over the years: Jimmy Durante, Johnny Horton, Merle Travis, Jim Reeves, Lawrence Welk, Patti Page, Danny Kaye, Buddy Holly and the Crickets. I made a record out in Clovis, New Mexico, and they [Buddy Holly and the Crickets] were my band. They hadn't recorded anything of their own at the time.

In Hollywood—I don't remember whether it was before or after the Big D Jamboree—I had a music teacher who knew Lawrence Welk very well. One day, Welk's secretary called and said he wanted to speak with me. This was just before he went on network TV. He asked me to come and have an interview with him.

He was very specific about moral standards. He wanted to know if I could work with that many guys and not be tempted. I said, "No problem." He was very Catholic and I was very Baptist. We went from his office down to the Aragon Ballroom, and he played the piano to accompany me. One by one, some of the guys in his group started joining in. First a drummer. Then a bass. And so on.

It felt less like an audition than a session. I did a ballad and an upbeat song for him. Then he asked me if I had a gimmick. Everybody wants to know if you've got a gimmick. I said, "Well, I yodel." He asked me to yodel for him. He just went nuts over that.

I drove back home through all the afternoon traffic in Hollywood—I lived in the San Fernando Valley—and didn't even get in the door before my sister came out on the porch and said, "Lawrence Welk is on the phone for you. He wants you to come in and work with him tonight." So I had to turn around and drive all the way back to Hollywood.

I worked with Mr. Welk on two or three occasions when his regular female vocalist couldn't make it. It was always on last-minute notice, but it was a pleasure to do it.

A girlfriend of mine told me about an opening with Esquivel in Las Vegas. It was part of a four-girl act. Esquivel could get more music out of six musicians and four girl singers than anybody I ever heard of.

I was straight out of First Baptist Church when I went to Vegas. I saw all those slot machines and took about six steps back. I was with Esquivel about three years. We were nine months out of the year at the Stardust and three months on the road.

I was working in Cocoa Beach, Florida, when Col. John Glenn made his space flight. I saw him take off. That rocket was gone just like that.

The astronauts used to always come into our club. They had their own special table. The manager told us not to ask for Col. Glenn's autograph when he came in. He wanted us to respect his privacy. We said, "Sure, OK."

So as I was coming down off the stage one night, Col. Glenn caught me by the arm and asked, "Do you do requests?" I said, "Well, yes sir, I do." And he said, "Would you sing 'Around the World'?" So I did.

When I came off the stage again, the manager was hot. He said,

"I told you not to bother that man." But I told him Col. Glenn had stopped me, not the other way around.

Of all the stars I worked with over the years, my favorite was Elvis Presley. I didn't work with him, I preceded him on his show. We did a Texas tour. He was so nice and so charming.

On the last night of the tour, he thanked me for being on the tour with him and being the kind of person I was. He said, "The guys tell me you're a Christian." I said, "Yes, I am." I felt sure I was going to be put down for that, as I had been many times before. But he said, "Well, don't ever change. Because if it weren't for my faith, I wouldn't be where I am today."

I thanked him for being considerate of me. He was so gracious.

Frances James, near a grave at Beeman Cemetery in Dallas, is known as 'the Cemetery Lady' because she has done so much to locate and help preserve early cemeteries in Dallas. Courtesy *The Dallas Morning News*, Ariane Kadoch, photographer.

Frances James

Frances James, seventy-seven, has lived in Dallas all her life. Over the past two decades, she has become known as the Cemetery Lady because of her efforts to save area pioneer burial places from destruction.

I was born in 1922. I grew up here in Dallas and went to Woodrow Wilson High School. I tell everybody I was born under the bridge, because where Thornton Freeway crosses over Lindsley Avenue is where our house was.

There were a lot of little frame houses there, and Mama and Daddy bought one back in 1920 after Daddy came back from the service. I have a picture of me when I was a little girl, standing by Daddy in his Army uniform. That was a big deal. November 11 of every year, Daddy put on his uniform.

We lived on Lindsley Avenue until 1928 and then we moved to a nicer house out at Hollywood, halfway between Tennison Park and the lake.

Daddy was a super salesman. But he sold road-building machinery. He was a partner in a company. When the Depression hit, there was no building going on. The counties, the state, nobody had the money to build anything.

So Daddy didn't make any money. We lost that house and had to move back down to the old frame house on Lindsley Avenue. Daddy had kept it for rent property. That was quite a comedown for us.

I got married before I was sixteen. I went to Woodrow the next year to enroll and the registrar told me I couldn't enroll because I was married. So I couldn't go to school. I didn't graduate.

But I love to study and I love to learn. My husband had gone to the University of Oklahoma, and all his books were in the house, and I would study them. I remember how excited I was when I took his algebra book and I could work the problems.

We had twenty-five years of a good life, and then we divorced. He decided to go do something else. I had two kids. I went to work for the telephone company. I worked there for twenty-seven years. I was single for six years.

My second husband I met through the telephone company. He worked for Western Electric. And we were married for twenty-five years. He died in 1993. He had diabetes. He was bedridden for a year and died here at home.

People call me the Cemetery Lady because I've probably talked to every newspaper and TV reporter in Dallas about cemeteries. Genealogical societies, historical societies, they all call me.

It started after I retired from the telephone company in '78. The people in the neighborhood where I lived then decided to have a neighborhood cleanup. Just two miles from where I lived there was a little pioneer cemetery, and we cleaned it up.

It was December 1, 1981. I remember because there was the grave there of a little lady who had died December 1, 1881. Exactly a hundred years before. We got rid of the brambles and the beer cans. The cemetery was between two churches, so there were lots of beer cans.

It was the Glover Cemetery. I had heard of the Texas historical markers, how the state has a procedure to erect markers for significant historical places. So I got together all the information to apply for a marker for the Glover Cemetery. And I got it. Then I got put on the Dallas County Historical Commission. I was on it from '83 till '89.

I did a whole bunch more Texas historical marker applications. I've done probably about fifty. Most of them were for cemeteries and churches. I found out a lot about all the different religions. They tell me I've done enough research to qualify for a thesis for a degree from a university.

Last spring, I did extensive research on the Pioneer Cemetery downtown. The city wants to expand the Convention Center into part of the cemetery. They did an excavation there and uncovered fifteen bodies. They moved them and reburied them in a dignified way, which is what you're supposed to do. You're not supposed to do it with a bulldozer and a backhoe, the way a lot of the real estate developers do if they think they can get away with it.

Protecting the cemeteries just kind of fell to me because nobody else was doing it. The cemetery laws in Texas are bad. All the law says is that it's illegal to desecrate or vandalize a cemetery. There's no enforcement, and a law that's not enforced is like no law at all. If I called the attorney general, I wouldn't get any help. If I called the sheriff, I wouldn't get any help. If I called the chief of police, I wouldn't get any help. They always say there's nothing they can do unless the culprit is caught in the act.

Publicity is really the only enforcement we have. Otherwise, the developers just bulldoze the graves and go on. They try to destroy a cemetery before anybody knows about it. I tell them, "These are human beings. In death, we're all equal. These people need to be protected." But by the time we put out one fire, another one has started.

Everyplace I go, I visit the old cemeteries. In Virginia City, Nevada, for instance, I went and found them on the side of a mountain. There were boys who were born in England, and they died at seventeen years old in the mines or some other place in Nevada, and I wondered if their mothers ever knew what happened to them. Probably not.

I've researched my family all the way back. Last September, I got to go to Germany and France, and I found my great-grandmother's cemetery in Ludz, Germany, a small village northeast of Berlin. I was thrilled about that. We cleaned the dead leaves off her grave.

I'm sure I'm the only one of her descendants who has visited her grave, for she had six children and they all came to the United States between 1870 and 1880.

The Boy Scouts are wonderful about helping us clean up our old cemeteries and set the tombstones back up. They're working on three or four right now.

I wrote to a member of a family whose cemetery the Boy Scouts had just cleaned up, and the lady just wrote a very brief thank-you note in reply. That family has no intention of taking care of that cemetery. The place where their mothers and fathers and grandparents are buried. All their ancestors.

It's a shame. In Dallas County, there are more than 200 of these little cemeteries. I'm not talking about Laurel Land and Hillcrest. These are the small ones. And we have history on just about all of them. They ought to be cared for.

Aki Shiratori of Dallas, proprietor of Images by Aki hair styling salon, works on his pottery at his home. Courtesy *The Dallas Morning News*, Michael Ainsworth, photographer.

Aki

Aki, fifty, is proprietor of Images by Aki, a hair-styling salon in Dallas. For many of the years he has lived here, he was an undocumented immigrant.

My real name is Hiroaki Shiratori. Hiro means "wise and clever." Aki means "bright and cheerful." Shiratori means "white swan." It's so long and difficult to say that I took "Aki" as a nickname. Also, during the time I was illegal, I didn't want to use my last name.

I was born in 1949, four years after the end of World War II, in Nagano Prefecture, where the Winter Olympics were held a few years ago. It's a beautiful mountain area of Japan.

When I was young, if I did something wrong, my parents would say, "American soldiers will come get you." I was scared, but I became curious about Americans.

After I graduated from high school, I went to a college in Tokyo. My degree is in art. I lived in Tokyo three more years before I moved here. Fifty years old I am now, and twenty-five years I've lived in the United States. It's amazing.

I had met my partner, this American guy. He was working in Japan, but he was from Dallas. I came back with him. I had wanted to come to the United States for a long time.

Even if I hadn't met him, I'm sure I would have come here. I saw the movie *West Side Story* when I was in junior high and I just loved it. I didn't know it was a Shakespeare story. I fell in love with Natalie Wood and Richard Beymer both. I thought, "My God, what beautiful people!" After that, I really wanted to come to the United States.

It was not easy to come here. Immigration was very tight. So I immigrated to Canada for seven months. Vancouver. But I just couldn't stand it. I was lucky enough to find a job immediately. I had a place to live immediately. But I didn't feel welcome. One time on the street, I was called 'Chink.' And I said, "I'm not 'Chink.' I'm 'Jap.'" I've never had that kind of experience in the United States.

Vancouver is a beautiful place, but I was lonely. I didn't know anybody. I wasn't doing what I wanted to do. I was doing architectural drafting. It was so easy. They would give me a job that was supposed to last a week and I would do it in one day. Most of the time, I didn't have anything to do. It made me crazy. Also, I missed my lover.

Then I came to Dallas. The first I had heard about Dallas was the assassination of Kennedy. I thought Dallas was a place that's hot all the time, in the middle of a desert, where everybody wears guns and owns oil wells.

When I arrived, I was surprised that Dallas was relatively cosmopolitan and a pretty big city, and a rich city. The people were very nice. The people in Dallas are good-looking, both men and women.

The city has changed a lot since I came here. It was very difficult to find Japanese food at first. Now you can even find a lot of the ingredients at the grocery store. That's a big difference.

I came on a travel visa. I had $250 when I arrived. My lover and I thought I should go to school. I considered becoming a veterinarian or a dog groomer or a hairdresser. I decided to be a hairdresser. I studied at Renee's Cosmetology Center and got my license.

I worked for three years in a salon, but I couldn't get my visa extended. I couldn't get a green card.

I got married. It was a marriage of convenience, to try to get a green card. It didn't work out. She divorced me, thank God. In 1979, I had to leave.

When I got back to Japan, I felt like I was dead. I felt I had left something of myself here in Dallas. I had to come back.

I knew I would be coming back as an illegal, so I told my parents that I loved them but I might not ever be able to come back, even if they were sick, even if they died. That was tough.

My parents understood. They told me not to come back to Japan if I was going to leave my heart in the United States. Amazing love.

I had to come back because the person I loved was over here. Also, I hadn't tried everything I wanted to. I was just a hairdresser, and that wasn't enough for me.

During the three years I had been in the United States, I was so busy surviving and trying to be accepted and trying to understand what people were saying, I didn't have time to become friends with anyone. But I had to come back. Life—especially gay life—is so much more open here. Any thought or opinion you have, you can express here.

In Japan, it's very difficult. They try to make you like everybody else. That makes it easier for a lot of people to live in a small space. So I came back to Dallas after only seven weeks in Japan.

I got in on a visitor's visa again and got my old job back. My love affair didn't work out, but because of that, I started working very hard. To forget.

I finally opened my own shop, Images by Aki. Twenty-one years ago. It was on Lower Greenville. Since then, I've moved up Greenville to Mockingbird. I had three shops at one time, and thirty or forty people working for me. Now I just have one shop. It's less headache. Much better for me. I'm getting old.

But I was illegal. When people in suits would walk in, I was scared to death. I thought they were coming after me. It was a really awful feeling, to be illegal.

I finally got a green card, thanks to President Reagan's amnesty. I was so scared to go apply for amnesty. I thought it was a trap. Now I've applied for citizenship, just this year. I'm excited. Right now, I feel that I don't have a country. I have a kind of floating-around feeling.

I feel really lucky. Lots of American people have accepted me. They gave me a chance. I'm really glad I came to Dallas, too. I love New York, but in New York I would be just another illegal alien. Anyway, there are too many people in a little space, like Japan. I have so many friends here, so many connections, so many opportunities.

For thirteen years, I've been doing pottery. For American people, my pottery has an Eastern feeling. For Japanese people, I'm very much Westernized. I'm going to have my first pottery show in Japan next year, in the Ginza in Tokyo. I sell it at the Dallas Museum of Art, at my house, and at my shop.

I donate that money to the AIDS Resource Center. Also, I volunteer to bring food to people with AIDS. Americans are such giving people. That's a big difference from the Japanese, I think. People here volunteer so much. I think that's wonderful.

My parents have been to visit me twice. Now that I have a green card, I go back to Japan every year. My father passed away four years ago. My first lover, who brought me here, passed away two years ago. He died young. He had heart problems. He was a silent partner in my business. We remained friends. He was a very important person to me. I miss him a lot.

I had a twelve-and-one-half-year love affair after him. He was HIV positive. He has AIDS now. He also does a lot of volunteer work for AIDS. I have myself tested regularly for HIV. I'm always so scared when I go to the mailbox to get the results. So far, I'm negative.

If I lived in Japan, I would try to be like everybody else, maybe, because it's easier to live that way. I would be more concerned about how I would be accepted by society. It's still a struggle here, but the United States is much better than Japan.

Here, individuality is very important. Spiritual growth is important. I can be vulnerable here, and it's OK. It's very difficult to be vulnerable in Japan. I am so glad to be here.

A Japanese publication recently asked me to write an article about my favorite city. At first, I wasn't thinking of choosing Dallas. Then I thought, "I've lived here for twenty-five years. It's an exciting city. I must like it." So I wrote about Dallas.

Yes, I love Dallas. Dallas is under my skin.

Ninety-one-year-old Etta Mayberry in front of the Magic Time Machine restaurant in Addison. The restaurant was formerly the old Addison School, where Mrs. Maberry attended as a child. Courtesy *The Dallas Morning News*, Joe Stefanchik, photographer.

Etta Maberry

The mural in the Dallas Area Rapid Transit station in Addison, Texas, includes a photo of the 1925 Addison High School girls basketball team. Etta Maberry, now ninety-one, is one of the girls in that picture. She attended the ceremony that opened the station.

I was two years old when my mother and daddy moved to a farm a few miles north of Addison. I started school at Hebron. I lived with my grandmother at that time so I wouldn't have to walk so far.

I lived at home the next year and went to the Possum Trot school. It was way out in the country. There was forty-two in the whole school. One teacher taught the first through the eighth grades.

I was about nine when I started school at Addison. I went there until I graduated. We lived at the time on a farm in a big old two-story house near the creek that moves right into the Frankford cemetery.

I didn't get to go to school the whole term because we had to chop cotton, and we had to pick cotton, and every time we did that, we had to stay out of school. So I had to do a lot of night studying.

We raised cotton and wheat and cows. My granddaddy had a syrup mill, so we raised sorghum cane. We had to strip the cane. We took a stick and knocked off the leaves. And we had to help run the syrup mill. My brother and I would turn the thing to grind the cane when the old horse got tired.

We had a big family. I was the oldest of ten. They didn't have a boy until the fourth one, so Dad used me a lot on the farm. I plowed. I drove cotton to the gin.

I had a team of mules then. Old Kate and Dinah. I'll never forget those mules. They would do anything I would tell them. They was just really good mules.

It was a wonderful life, in a way. We had a big orchard. We raised all of our food except sugar and coffee.

But it was hard. I never did have a childhood. I had to start taking care of the kids. There was one every two years. When I married, I had a sister who was just two months old. I was eighteen.

I went to junior college at Arlington twice in the summertime and took music. Arlington then was just a three-story building. It was part of Texas A&M. By the time I was fourteen or fifteen, I was playing the piano for the church. I played all the marches for the school.

My daddy was a deacon in the church. And, you know, in the Baptists you couldn't go to dances. Daddy was strict. We could have company to come to our house, but we never could go to other people's houses to a party.

So when I got up in high school, my grandmother—they was Methodists—would call my mother and say, "We've got some sewing for Etta to do," and I would go down there and we would go to the party. That was the only parties I ever got to go to.

Addison wasn't nothing in those days. There was a Baptist church and a Methodist church. On the corner was a dry goods store run by the Atkins. Our post office was in that store. On the other street there was a bank and a grocery store, and there was the depot. Up one side of that street was five houses and the gin. And up the other side was four houses. There was two houses behind the church and one house over on the other side. And that was Addison.

It was a good place. You never heard of robbing. You never heard of anyone shooting anybody or running over anybody. It was a nice, quiet little town. Everybody went to church. And, of course, the whole gang went to school. Tenth grade was as high as it went. My family had five kids in school at once.

Addison School is gone now. The building is a restaurant. I like to go there and eat and pretend I'm back in school.

I graduated the 9th of June in 1926, and I married the 15th. Charles Maberry. He worked in the drugstore there in Addison. We moved to Dallas the day we were married. He went to work for Corrugated Box Company and I went to work for Brown's Candy and Cracker Company. I dipped chocolates. It was down in the West End, where the Old Spaghetti Warehouse is now.

Oh, I tell you, I was scared to death to be in Dallas. That was something unusual. Then I got pregnant and had to quit. Then I went to work for a while in a shop that sold knickknacks.

My daddy introduced me to a man out at Love Field. Byron Good. He was a good friend of my daddy, and he was running a school for aviators out there. The Army had given it up, and Byron Good took it over.

My husband got the drugstore there, called Airway Drugstore. On Denton Drive. He was the pharmacist. There were eight rooms up above it, so we opened a rooming house up there. I had a cook and a housekeeper. All of my boarders were aviators.

Every time one of them graduated from aviator school, I had to go up with him. I would tell my husband one of the aviators was graduating, and he would say, "Oh, my God! I'll start praying!" The planes were just old jennies. Some of them had been in the war and they were pretty ragged. I took my son up there once. He was two years old. They tied him in the seat with me.

I had my rooming house for about three years and then it all went *phhhht!* This was 1929. You know what happened in 1929. The aviators all went home. I even had to pay some of their ways home. The drugstore closed. It was a sad time.

Charles couldn't hold a job. He couldn't find one. So we separated. I went to my mother's and he went to Kansas City to work as a service manager for the Hoover vacuum cleaner company.

My mother lived at Perryton, Texas. Way out in the Panhandle. I would never go there again. That was the worst place I ever went in my life. My parents had the biggest wheat crop you ever saw. I hauled wheat for a whole month. I plowed. I worked the whole time I was there.

I'm telling you, those tumbleweeds would come blowing down, and you would think the world was coming to an end. You would look up and the sky would be as black as it could be, just rolling. I felt like I was smothering.

I wouldn't want to live out there. Not me. Unh-unh. I wrote my husband and told him how terrible it was and he wrote my daddy and told him to put us on the train to Kansas City.

I went to work for Nellie Don, a dress factory in Kansas City, and learned designing. A year and a half later, my husband was transferred to Iowa.

On the way up there, we saw this grocery store for sale in Kirksville, Missouri. I said, "Stop!" We went in and looked the store over. I said to my husband, "You go on. I'm going to stay here." I had decided to buy the store. I paid down on it. It had a three-room house in the back. I lived in that. My husband was traveling over five states. I didn't see him once for three months.

The store had good trade, but I got homesick. I had been away for three years and hadn't seen nobody. None of my people. So when my husband came home, I said, "What do you think of just packing up and going back to Dallas?" And he said, "I was thinking the same thing."

So he settled up with the Hoover company and we got in the car and drove all night long to Perryton. I tell you, that West Texas! We was there about two weeks, and then we came on to Dallas.

He went to work for Johnson Chevrolet and I went to work for the Marcy Lee dress factory. I knew how to make patterns. I knew how to cut. Pretty soon, I wasn't making dresses, I was making styles, because of what I had learned at Nellie Don.

I worked there, I guess, five years. Then another dress factory offered me $50 a week more to come over there. I worked for six different dress factories.

One of the men I worked for would run short of money for the payroll and he would send me over to the Carousel Club to get it from Jack Ruby. Ruby always gave it to me in cash. He wouldn't give us a check.

When my boss got the money to pay Ruby back, I would carry it to him. Always cash. Ruby was a gangster. Nothing but a gangster.

I worked fifty-five years in the clothing business. When I retired in 1988, I was eighty years old. That's a long time to slave. I never got to be a child.

Lindon Dodge broke his neck in a diving accident when he was twenty-one. He tutors high school students, is an amateur astronomer, a guitar player, and builds and flies radio-controlled model airplanes. Courtesy *The Dallas Morning News*, Randy Eli Grothe, photographer.

Lindon Dodge

Lindon Dodge, thirty-eight, has been a paraplegic for seventeen years. He lives with his dog, Fred, in Midlothian. He tutors high school students in English and history.

I was twenty-one years old when I had my accident. It was just one of those things. I went to Lake Waxahachie with some friends of mine. We went off to a part of the lake that I wasn't familiar with, and I picked the wrong spot to dive off of. I hit something under the water and broke my neck. I've been this way since then.

I can't describe how it felt, but I'll never forget it. It was like all the feeling in my body just drained out my feet and left me. It's like it might still be down there in a hole in the water. I couldn't stand up. I couldn't get my head above water. I was drowning.

After a while, I went into shock. I was lying there in the cold water and my body temperature went down. I guess my circulation just went bad. I would be dead if one of my friends hadn't come in after me. I was unconscious for a few days.

I found out pretty quick I wasn't going to walk anymore. Doctors don't waste any time letting you know that kind of stuff. They told me I could start planning on a new life. They told me I was going to be living in a wheelchair.

I got my hands back. I was without my hands for the first couple of years. They never gave me much hope of getting them back, but I did. That was miraculous in itself, I think. I know what it's like to not be able to strike a lighter or brush my teeth or feed myself, all those things that you can't imagine not doing. When I could make an A chord on my guitar for the first time, I knew my hands were going to be OK.

I decided I was going to learn to do as many things for myself as I could. Get in and out of the wheelchair. Get in and out of cars. I've had good teachers. People like Jim Hayes and Casey Caudle and my best friend, Robert Murray, who are in the same situation I am. They showed me how to learn by trial and error to get through life the best I could. They've taught me more than the therapists could, because the therapists have never gone through it.

Robert taught me that you've got to laugh, man. He taught me to have humility about it, to accept that this is the way things are. It's not fun. It's not pleasant. But you can't sit around and whine the rest of your life.

If the doctors would tell me, "We can give you back your bladder function, your bowel function and any one part of the body that you choose," I would say that I'm cured. But all the doctors have been able to do is rearrange my organs to facilitate life in a wheelchair. They don't really fix anything.

Some people don't understand that I still have a life. It's just not like theirs. One woman told me that I'm a waste of skin. I try not to let that kind of stuff bother me.

Before the accident, I had some pretty good stuff going on. I was working out here at the steel mill. It was one of the best jobs I've had. It was hard work. Hot. Dangerous. But I used to enjoy going to work.

I was learning to fly airplanes. I was going to school at Mountainview.

I got my degree in English and history at the University of Texas at Arlington after the accident. I tutor kids in English and history. I could be a schoolteacher, but it would be hard to handle thirty kids at a time. I build and fly model airplanes with a buddy of mine. I play guitar. I read. I try to write, but I'm not very good at it.

I've got three old cars that I try to keep running, but that's more aggravating than anything else. I know what I need to do, but I can't do it because I can't stand up.

I love auto racing. I go to a lot of races. I'd go to all of them if I could. I've been to the Texas Motor Speedway every year since it opened.

Astronomy has fascinated me since I was a kid. I have a little eight-inch telescope. I keep up with the McDonald Observatory Web site on my computer. Images they've taken of the universe.

During my lifetime, I've seen a total change in what the astronomers believe the universe to be. It's totally different from when I was a kid. It's a good time to be alive for an amateur astronomer. More advances have been made in the last couple of decades than in the last thousand years.

If I could just work at that observatory. If I could just sweep the floor, just to be around those big telescopes. Geez. They wouldn't even have to pay me.

I would like to see some of the world. I would like to go to Israel. Jerusalem. I love all that ancient history. I almost feel I need to go. Not just there, but several places. For some reason, something calls me to southern France. I don't know what's there, but I want to go, man.

But I couldn't leave Fred here alone. He's fourteen years old, and he's had some problems of his own. He was paralyzed last year for a while. I had to carry him around in a wagon.

If I hadn't had my accident, I probably would be living the life everybody else does. Get up, go to work, come home, watch TV, get up, go to work, come home, watch TV. I don't see my life being much different than anyone else's. I was young. I didn't really have any plans, but I sure didn't paint this picture.

My only ambition is to get out of this situation, but time is running out on that. I know I'm stuck in this wheelchair.

I hate it more every day that I live in it. But I know that's the way it is.

Blues singer R. L. Griffin owns Blues Palace II in South Dallas. Courtesy *The Dallas Morning News*, Randy Eli Grothe, photographer.

R. L. Griffin

R. L. Griffin, fifty-eight, is the proprietor of Blues Palace II at the corner of Meadow Street and Grand Avenue in South Dallas. He has been singing the blues in Dallas for more than twenty years.

My home is Kilgore, down in East Texas. My father worked at a cleaners there. He was a presser. He pressed clothes. My mom worked at a cleaners also. That was their job: working at cleaners. Growing up, I used to caddy a lot. I fell in love with golf. And I had a job at a restaurant three or four times.

From there, I stuck with music. I went to school at C. B. Dansby. Now it's Kilgore High. The inspiring that I got to be a musician was from my band director at the time, Rufus B. Anderson. You know how when you're in school you always want to become a football player? But Rufus Anderson steered me in a different direction. He was letting me know that even if I didn't make it in football, I could always play music.

So that was my goal. I started out playing drums. I didn't know I was a singer until one day in the chapel there Mr. Anderson asked me to sing a song. That was during the time when Little Willie John was very, very popular and had put out "Fever," so I did that song in the chapel. Everybody was hollering for me, so they made me think that I was a singer, and that's when I started singing. I was fourteen, fifteen years old, something like that.

After high school, I married Daisy, who I met at a basketball game in Tyler. I came to Dallas and started working with a group here, Big Beau Thomas and the Arrows. I worked with them down in old North Dallas at a club called Delmonico's, over in the State-Thomas neighborhood.

I was singing then. I got up off the drums and started being a stand-up vocalist. I stayed there with Big Beau until I got my own group. When I got my own group, I started playing at a club in Dallas called the Red Jacket. It was in North Dallas off of San Jacinto. At the time, it was just an all-white club. Blacks weren't going to it at the time. It was strictly white.

It was very segregated in those days. The onliest black I knew who would come over to the Red Jacket was John Wiley Price. He was going to SMU. All of the students from SMU was coming to that club. I think the Red Jacket is out on Greenville now. A friend of mine I knew in school owns it. His name is John.

I was making my living playing music. When I first started out, I had another job, but pretty soon I put my full time into playing music. Over at the Red Jacket, I was working every night. We was off on Monday nights, but worked all the rest. When I was with Big Beau Thomas, we worked every night but Monday, plus we did two matinees. We would do a matinee on Sunday evening from about four o'clock till about seven. Then we would come back and do another one from seven till about eight-thirty or nine. Then we would go to the club and work.

I played with some of the top entertainers. I played with the late and great Z. Z. Hill. I played with Johnnie Taylor. I played with Little Milton and the late and great Freddy King. I've been on the show with B. B. King. I played with all the top entertainers around.

So I've kind of been around for a while. Over the last twenty years, I've played most all the clubs here in Dallas. I do a lot of private parties in different hotels downtown. And most of the entertainers that come to town, I'm the one that's been opening up the shows for them.

My band is Hal Harris and His Show Band. They've been with me a good fifteen years. I sing with them. Hal Harris is my bandleader. My guitar player's name is Jerry Jones. He's been with me now about five years. As the saying says, he's a tough white boy. We get along real good. He's a nice person. The drummer's name is Charles Miles, the keyboard is Raymond Green and I have another singer that's Harold Walker.

We play to a mixed crowd here, and everybody has really been in our corner. We haven't had no problems at this club. Everything's just been fine.

It was almost exactly thirteen years ago that I opened my first club, Blues Palace. It's still across the street there. We kind of outgrew that club. We moved over here about a year ago. It's a much bigger place. We have more room for everything.

I just finished a new CD. It's called *Too Hot to Stop*. It's on Riot Records. It's in all the record stores. Three years ago I played over in England and over there in Amsterdam. I had a great time over there. And now I'm a DJ at the radio station KKDA. My time is from seven o'clock until ten every night. I've been doing it just a year and I've really been enjoying it.

At the club here, I work Thursday through Sunday. We have good crowds. We don't have the young crowd here. We have the old adult crowd that likes the blues. We play contemporary blues. We don't do the low-down gut blues, but we mix it up some. We do some of the Jimmy Reed and the Lightnin' Hopkins. And we update it a little bit with some of the Johnnie Taylors and the Little Miltons and the Greg Smiths. And some T-Bone Walker and Blind Lemon Jefferson.

People love the blues. When the blues started out, people sang the blues because they had problems and singing the blues made them forget their problems. Back in the days when the blacks was out in the field working, they didn't have anything else they could do, so they would go to singing and it would make their day pass away. That's what gave all of them the blues.

Contemporary blues is different from the old blues because we changed the beat. The rhythm part is about the same, but we gave the blues a more up-to-date beat. We keep it on the one. When you keep it on the one, that means you never speed up for nothing.

You just keep it right on the one. [He sings:] *My baby's gone. My baby's gone. She left me this morning* . . . See, everything is still on the one.

Stuff like B. B. King would do. He can play those low blues, but he also does the up-to-date blues. You're still singing the blues. You're still singing about somebody done you wrong, or you can't wait till tomorrow to find a million dollars or something like that. You just pick up your tempo a little bit.

All kinds of blues singers come in here to perform. I've had Bobby Rush. I've had Little Milton. I've had Greg Smith, Buddy Myers, Ernie Johnson, guys like that. Most entertainers that's been doing something have been here. People with records that have been doing pretty good. I knew all these entertainers before they even got hits. I knew them at the time they was just getting started, like myself. So we always kind of fall back and help each other.

We present the blues in a safe, clean atmosphere. The neighborhood has been real nice, over here in South Dallas. I have the largest club and the safest club. We seat 200 people in here. We have only beer and wine. We're what you call a BYOB club. I have six security people that work here. And you have to be a certain age to come in. You've got to be twenty-five on up. We don't let teenagers in. You have to be grown. And you have to show your ID.

Young people can't handle themselves. Their mind is confused about a lot of different things. I feel that if I go with the older crowd, these people should have some kind of sense. And it has been like that. I've been blessed that I haven't had any problems.

But young people love the blues, too. When we play overseas, that's what we play to, the young audience. What they're doing, they're studying the blues over in England. They have classes, just like we go to a regular class at school. They have classes about the blues. And those kids over there really turn on to it.

Even here in Dallas, the young people like the blues. When we do outdoor concerts, we get the young and the old. It's just in the club scene where you can't let the kids come in. The blues is doing good among the young.

I've been doing a lot of things in the neighborhood. One thing that kind of made me stand out around here is that around Christmastime I always have a drive here at the club to take care of those who can't afford to get their kids anything for Christmas. I always do that. At Thanksgiving, I always give away from 100 to 150 turkeys in the neighborhood. Anybody that comes by. I've been doing these things in the neighborhood ever since I've been here.

I feel like I'll be blessed if I do the right thing. And the Lord has blessed me. All my life, I've been doing what I love best, all the livelong day. All my life.

Dr. Herbert Shore was the first gerontologist in Dallas and has worked with the elderly in the city for more than fifty years. Courtesy *The Dallas Morning News*, Jim Mahoney, photographer.

Herbert Shore

*Dr. Herbert Shore, seventy-four, may have been
the first trained gerontologist in Dallas. After
nearly forty years as an administrator of a home
for the elderly and nearly thirty years as a
professor at the University of North Texas, he's a
widely known consultant on aging.*

The Greeks had a god for old age. His name was Geras. Geriatrics is the medical study of aging. Gerontology is a bigger umbrella. It includes all aspects of aging—the economic, social, psychological. Gerontology is the science of old age.

I'm a gerontologist, and this year marks fifty years that I have worked with the elderly. It has been a long career, and I've been the luckiest man alive. Every day of those fifty years, I've worked with older people, shared their joys and sorrows and problems and happiness. There's never been a dull moment.

I was born and raised in New York City. I'm a damn Yankee. But I'm a Texan by choice. People used to call me a "Texicated Yankee." In 1944 I went into the Army and was assigned to the Air Corps and wound up in San Antonio. I spent two-and-one-half-years there.

Back in New York, I was dating Selma, the lady I later married. We've been married for fifty-one years now. And on the back of my letters to her I would put the initials LSMFT, which in those days meant "Lucky Strike Means Fine Tobacco." But if you were in the service, LSMFT meant "Lord, Save Me From Texas."

When I was discharged in November 1946, I said I would never, never, never, never, never, never set foot in Texas again. The lesson from that is, never say never. Little did I know that seven years later I would get an invitation to come to Dallas to open the Dallas home for the Jewish aged, which is known as Golden Acres.

In 1953, when I got the invitation to come here, I was assistant administrator of a large home in Chicago. Selma and I were both damn Yankees. We had an eight-month-old daughter. We thought Texas was, you know, South, and we didn't want to live in the South. We didn't realize that Texas is actually Southwest.

We came up with a five-year plan. If I succeeded in Dallas in five years, I would move up and go somewhere else; if I failed, I would find something else to do.

I may have been the first professionally trained gerontologist in Dallas. I got my master's at Columbia University. When I went to Columbia in 1949, I was the first student to ask to work with the elderly.

My wife was a schoolteacher. We lived in Manhattan, right in the theater district. Selma would travel up to the Bronx to teach public school, and I was working as a recreation director in a community center in Brooklyn, working with kids. She left the house at seven in the morning to be at work at eight. I left the house at two to be at work at three. I got home at midnight. We would leave notes on the table: "See you Tuesday at two o'clock, maybe."

Seniors went to the community center during the day, when the kids weren't there. It was the first senior center in the United States. It had opened during the war. I said to myself, "Anybody can work with kids. But who's interested in the old folks?"

So I decided that's what I would do. I began to see that old people not only could do a great deal for themselves, but they could do a great deal for others as well. They had a lot of knowledge and wisdom that others could benefit from.

That's what the Senior Citizens of Greater Dallas, which I helped establish, is all about today. They have eleven programs where older people go to hospitals and work with babies who had drug-addict parents, things like that.

Anyway, I came to Dallas in 1953 and I opened Golden Acres, intending to stay five years. Well, at the end of five years they were enlarging the home, so I stayed. I wound up retiring from Golden Acres after thirty-eight years.

I came to a fifty-bed, small home for the elderly. I left with a major retirement community with all the components—nursing home, independent living for retired people, a senior center, everything. When I left, we had 550 people living on the campus. So Selma and I raised our three children here in Dallas.

For thirty-eight years, one afternoon a week, I also was an academician at North Texas State University, where I got my doctorate. I taught undergraduate sociology there for ten years, and for twenty-eight years I prepared administrators for retirement communities and long-term care facilities. So I had the opportunity not only to work with older people, but also interface with young students. That's the best of all possible worlds. I trained over 1,000 administrators.

My value to the university was that I was a practitioner. I did it every day. I met the payroll, I knew how to choose employees, I knew how to work with the board.

I've also had a career as a public servant. As I said, I was one of the founders of the Senior Citizens of Greater Dallas and later had the privilege of being its president. Mayor Annette Strauss appointed me chair of the Senior Affairs Commission of the city of Dallas. I also was on several national boards. I'm still on one national board in Washington and several advisory committees.

I was one of the founders and past president and an active board member of Community Homes for Adults Inc., which operates group homes for mentally retarded adults. The state agencies were throwing them out, and they had no place to go. So we created this organization. That was a great joy in my life.

So I've had three or four careers. My family's favorite joke is that I've flunked retirement.

Being old is a lot different now from what it was fifty years ago. Now, the sky's the limit for older people. They go to college and write books and create music and do volunteer work.

The image of the elderly as decrepit and unfunctional has really changed. There's a much greater appreciation of older people today. They don't have to be put on a shelf. Now a man like Ronald Reagan can be president of the United States.

I'm fortunate in that I lived through and witnessed the growth of gerontology as a profession and as a career. I became a fellow in the Gerontological Society of America, which is the umbrella organization of professionals, in 1952. That's a long time ago.

I'm a consultant now. My students all over the country still call on me. I do a lot of consulting, because the changes in health care are moving so quickly that professionals who deal with the elderly can't be reactive anymore, they have to be proactive. They've got to position themselves for the future. I do a lot of board and staff education.

Only five percent of the elderly are living in institutions at any given time now. Most older people can and want to live independently in their own homes.

And the hottest thing going today is assisted living, for people who need some minimal supervision and assistance. Unfortunately, we're getting to the point where there's an assisted-living home on every corner, like gas stations. They're being overbuilt. It's a feeding frenzy. People are living longer. A significant part of the population is over eighty. There are going to be more centenarians around.

The big question is: Can you save enough during your work life to support you during a longer retirement life? It's an issue of planning. You can't start saving for your retirement when you're sixty years old. Nowadays you have to start thinking about that when you're thirty.

There are also quality-of-life issues. What are you going to do with the time that you have? We're rethinking, redefining retirement nowadays. It's taking on whole new meanings. Some people may not want to retire. They shouldn't have to.

We're going to have to make some changes in Social Security

and Medicare, or the boomers are going to have a wake-up call. They're crazy if they think they're going to be able to depend on Social Security alone. The boomers should not be in denial. They're going to live a long time. That means they have to do some planning.

But now is a good time to be old. I've really had a very wonderful career.

Holocaust survivor Leo Laufer endured thirteen slave labor camps including Auschwitz, where he was tattooed. Courtesy *The Dallas Morning News*, Ariane Kadoch, photographer.

Leo Laufer

Leo Laufer, seventy-seven, is the only member of his family who survived the Holocaust. He has lived in Texas for fifty years.

I was born in the city of Lodz, Poland, of an ultra-Orthodox Jewish family. There were eight children. I was number four. My father was in the textile business, but it was very mediocre. Absolutely nothing. He was a strong believer in God and all his disciples, the rabbis. We were very poor.

We lived in two rooms. Ten people. We had to pump water in the yard. We had no toilet facilities. If you had to go at midnight, you had to go in the yard, two flights down. We had no gas. We had to chop wood. We also used coal.

But it was a loving family. We were very, very, very close. I had a brother who was a year and a half older than I. He died in 1938 of appendicitis. He went into the hospital one day and never got out. He's the only brother I had who is buried in a cemetery. Another brother had married and moved out of our rooms. He had a wife and three small children. So when the war started, in 1939, there were only eight of us living in the two rooms.

We lived in the same neighborhood where the Nazis built the ghetto, so we didn't have to move. Before the ghetto closed, we were victims not only of the Germans who had invaded Poland, but of our own neighbors, our own Christian, Catholic believers.

I'll tell you an example. Across the street from us, there was a bakery. After the war started, we had to stay in line practically all night, until six o'clock in the morning when the bakery opened up, to get a loaf of bread. Since we had a large family, my brothers and sisters and I took turns standing in line. We would stand for an hour or two, and then switch.

Our neighbors used to pull us out of the line. They would say, "You're a Jew. You don't have to eat." We could feel the hatred from both sides, from the Germans and from our neighbors.

My father was scared to death to go down to the street. The collaborators, some of the people from our city, used to go around with the Germans and show them the windows where the Jews lived, and they would drag them out. One time, before they formed the ghetto, they dragged out my father and practically pulled his beard out of his face. He was livid and shameful. He tied a handkerchief over his face so we couldn't see the scars.

On May 31, 1940, the Germans formed the ghetto. They put up barbed wire around it, and gates. If you were a Jew and didn't live inside the ghetto, you had to move into it. The last street in the ghetto was our street. Across the fence in the back of the yard of our apartment house was where the Christians lived. They could go wherever they wanted. We couldn't. But I said, "Thank God. We can be alone with our own people."

Then we started to get hungry. I was seventeen, going on eighteen. I saw that if I didn't do something, something was going to happen. My family was going to get sick. They were going to starve.

I had some friends who were Christians, who were Gentiles, who were Catholics. As a youngster, I used to play ball in the street with them like any other kid. There was a woman whose son was a very good friend of mine. Her husband was in the Polish army. Their son was about my age.

I took the risk to run across the barbed wire and struck up a conversation with this Mrs. Stanislava Grabowska, a precious woman. I said to her, "We are starving from hunger. Is there any way that you can help us smuggle in through the barbed wire a loaf of bread, a pound of butter?" I said, "Whatever you want, we will pay you."

She consented. Try to imagine the barbed wire. There was a German guard at the end of the street and another one at the other end. Mrs. Grabowska would drive by in her buggy and throw the bundle of food over the wire at a predetermined place, and I would grab it and throw the money back, tied to a stone. I would have to sell half or more of it to get the money for her. The rest was for my family.

For a few months, it was beautiful. I had more food than I had had before the war. We started in the latter part of June, and through July and August and part of September, everything was absolutely fine.

Until one day she drove through and threw her package, and I picked it up, and I was grabbed in the back by two men. They were Gestapo. They grabbed me and took me to the police station, across the street from the biggest Catholic church in Lodz. They started interrogating me, trying to find out who the woman was who was smuggling food into the ghetto.

I thought, "If I say I don't know, maybe they will let me go." I stayed in this Gestapo place about ten days. They were beating me terribly every night, trying to get Mrs. Grabowska's name. I kept on saying I didn't know. They kept on beating me. Finally, I wound up in a hospital. I was really bruised up. My behind, my back, my shoulders, everything. But they never found out who the woman was.

I thought everything was going to be all right. I came home. Some of the furniture had been broken up for fire. There was no food. My little sisters are starving. I said, "I'm going to try it again." I went across the barbed wire and told Mrs. Grabowska what had happened. We started over again.

It lasted maybe two to three weeks. One night in the latter part of October of 1940, two men from the Gestapo came to the house around midnight. My father opened the door. They hit him. He fell all the way to the other side of the room. They asked, "Where is Leib?" My Jewish name is Leib. I changed it to Leo when I came to the States.

They went to the bed where I was and told me to put my clothes on and come fast.

Schnell! Schnell! So they took me away. I left my father, my mother, my four sisters and one brother.

They took me to a place where they had people already in custody. After two days, they took us to the railroad station. We didn't know where we were going. They loaded us into two cattle cars and transported us out of Lodz.

There were about 100 people in each car. They took us to a city called Poznan, which was a large city, but not as big as Lodz or Warsaw. We saw farm wagons pulled by horses. They put us in these wagons and drove us for another two to three hours to a very remote area called Ruchotski-Mlyn. "Mlyn" in Polish means "mill."

As we drove into this farm, we could see a big barn made out of brick that would have held about 100 cattle. There was another big barn nearby and a little brick house where the farmer lived. To the right of the barn was a water mill like you see in Belgium or Holland and a river called Dolca. The blades were turning. It was a mill to grind corn. We were happy when we saw this thing. We thought, "Oh, my gosh, we'll have bread at least."

We got out of the wagons and lined up, and we saw several civilians with swastikas and rifles. They told us to go to one of the barns and get some shovels that were there. We got the shovels and they took us into this big barn and we cleaned out the manure. Evidently, the cows just left. They didn't give us any hoses to wash it down. After we cleaned it up as good as we could, they told us to bring bales of hay and lay the hay on the ground over the manure.

This became our lodging from October of 1940 until early February of 1941. The work we did was straightening the channel of the Dolca River. Wherever there was a bend in the river, we filled it in so it would go smooth. The owner of the mill was a Pole of German descent. His name was Buda.

When we left, less than half of us had survived. It was not from malnutrition. We had as much bread as we wanted and as much soup as we wanted. And they were all young men, eighteen to twenty-two. They died from being infected by lice. We didn't take one single shower during the months we were there. We were sleeping on straw, on the manure. Everything stank. And it was winter. I didn't have any gloves. The clothes I had were the clothes I had grabbed in the house when I was arrested.

We became so immune to what we were seeing. Sometimes our friends would fall into the river and freeze to death. We would fish them out, throw them on a wagon, bring them back home to the barn, pitch them into a ditch in back of the barn and cover them up. We didn't have any feeling anymore. There was no crying or moaning or howling or feeling. Nothing. Everybody was waiting for his own death.

Some of the boys had more courage than I did. You could scrape hundreds of lice off your body. Somebody accumulated a bunch of lice and one day, when they opened up the gate in the morning, threw them on the guards.

The guards were civilians. Poles of German descent. One day we told them we weren't going to work, that we wanted to see a doctor. We were scared to death. We thought they were going to kill us. But we had scars and infected open wounds from the lice. Already more than 100 had died.

Two days later, a doctor came. He was German and had a big mustache. He didn't want to come in where we were. He told us to come out of the barracks, and he stood on the other side of the barbed wire from us. He was twenty or thirty feet from us. He told us to take our pants down, and he looked at our wounds. Then he said something about "quarantine" and told us to go back in the barn.

A few days later, the wagons came again. They closed the camp and took us to Poznan and put us in a stadium where they used to play soccer. At the time we left the farm, we ninety or so survivors thought we were the only Jews from the ghetto who had been incarcerated. But in this stadium were thousands of people from all different little cities.

We told them our story and they told us theirs. The stadium was a quarantine place. We didn't go to work. They gave us one bowl of soup and one piece of bread in the morning. We walked around and around in the stadium, like in an insane asylum.

When we arrived, the field had been covered with grass. By the time we left—I think it was less than a month—you couldn't find a single blade of grass. When we got the soup, we picked grass and shredded it and put it in the soup to thicken it. We thought it would nourish us. Instead, we got diarrhea, we got all kinds of diseases. A lot of kids died.

Finally, they chose 100 to 150 of the strongest survivors to go to work. The first place was Eichenwald. "Wald" means "forest." It was a town cut out of the forest. We were building a highway and a railroad from Poznan to Warsaw. We were supervised by civilians with boots, swastikas, rifles. We never saw a German soldier at all from 1940 until 1943. It was all civilians. As we finished five or ten miles, we took the same barracks and moved it farther down the line. I made about seven of these camps.

We didn't know until after the war how this German machine worked. We weren't chained together. Some of us might have been able to run away. But the Germans notified the people in the area where we were working that these were Jewish prisoners. They offered rewards for informing on runaways. Maybe two pounds of sugar or a pound of butter or a carton of cigarettes.

So the civilians who lived in those little towns were watching for us to run away. Two boys from our group ran away. They brought them back a couple of days later.

I've never seen these little camps reported in the books and documentaries. They're all about Auschwitz, Buchenwald, and the other concentration camps. But there were thousands and thousands of little camps across the countryside from 1940 until the

Russians started coming into Poland around 1943 or '44. Then the Germans shut down all the little camps and put all the people in Auschwitz, Buchenwald, and the others.

The atrocities in those little camps were sometimes worse than they were in the concentration camps. They had these trucks they called "delousing trucks." They were like cement-mixer trucks, but they had chemicals in them. Every weekend, they took our clothes and put them in there to get rid of the lice.

So when they caught these two boys who had run away, they lined us up for a ceremony. One by one, they took the two boys, put them in the truck with the chemicals and turned on the steam. Ten minutes later, they took them out and put them on the ground, and we all had to walk by and look at them.

Their heads were blown up. Their arms were shriveled. They didn't look human. It was the most horrible thing I had ever seen. They told us that's what would happen to us if we tried to escape.

I stayed in this camp until 1943. On August 23, we came to Auschwitz-Birkenau. Birkenau is three miles from Auschwitz. I was actually in Birkenau. From the 1,500 and some-odd who came in with me, less than 1,000 went to the labor camps. The rest went to the crematorium.

Hundreds of thousands of people were in Birkenau, in Camp A, Camp B, Camp C, Camp D; Camp E was the Gypsies. We came into Birkenau at night. When we got out of the railroad car, we saw dogs and, for the first time, German soldiers. Nice-looking young men. Six foot tall. Handsome. We didn't know anything about the crematorium. We didn't see it. I was assigned to a certain group, and the next day we went to work.

To be honest, not knowing about the crematorium, not knowing what was happening at Auschwitz, it was like going from hell to heaven. At the other camps, we had Ukrainians, Latvians, Lithuanians, and Estonians guarding us. They were the meanest people I ever saw in my whole life. When we came to Auschwitz, every hair was shaved, we were showered and cleaned up, and we came out like a survived human being. They gave us striped uniforms and put a tattoo on our arms.

It seemed like a normal procedure. But then we found out we were surrounded by electric wires. If you just touch it, you're gone. And when we walked out the gate to go to work, there was this big orchestra playing classical music. An orchestra of twenty or twenty-five people. It was unbelievable. Playing beautiful music as we were going out to work and coming in.

And over the gate was a sign: *Arbeit macht Frei*, which means "Work makes free." Then I looked to my left, and I saw these chimneys blowing out fire. And I asked what the horrible smell was, and they told me it was from human flesh.

In 1943 and '44, I worked building more barracks. Life didn't mean a thing. We knew we weren't going to survive. Our camp was Camp D. Camp D was the big labor force. We were all men. There were quite a few thousand people. Then there was a ditch and the electric barbed wire, and then there was Camp E, where the Gypsies were.

They were all there. Families. Men, women, children. They were all there together. We used to listen to them play music after we got home from work. One night in the fall of '44, there was a commotion at Camp E. When we lined up the next morning, Camp E was totally empty.

The Gypsies had gone to the crematorium. They burned them all. Fathers, mothers, babies, grandparents. Everybody was gone. And a rumor started that the last transport of Jews from the Lodz ghetto was going into Camp E.

Sure enough, a few days later, a new transport comes in. We come in from work and we see a new world. Camp E is occupied by many thousands of people. Of course, everybody who came from Lodz went to the barbed wire and tried to find a loved one or a friend. The screaming was unbelievable. There was about twenty feet distance between our barbed wire and Camp E's. I screamed, "Laufer! Laufer!" All of a sudden, somebody showed up at the barbed wire, and I finally recognized my older brother Szmerl, the one who was married.

Our conversation was all in screaming. He asked me, "Where's my wife and children?" I knew there was no chance they had gone to the labor force. They must have gone to the crematorium. So I said, "Szmerl, I don't know where they went." Then I asked him, "What happened to the rest of our family?" I had left in 1940, and this was the end of 1944. This was the first chance I had had to ask anyone about my family in all that time. He said, "They took them away in 1942." I said, "Where?" He said, "I don't know."

For ten or twelve days, we saw each other at the barbed wire, and our conversation was always the same: "Where is my wife?" and "Where is my family?" There was nothing else left to talk about.

Then one night I came and he was gone. I found out after the war that he had been transported to Dachau and died there in January 1945. If he had stayed in Auschwitz until January, he would have survived. That's when the Russian army liberated Auschwitz.

In the latter part of '44 I was taken to Sachsenhausen. It's near Berlin. I worked in an airplane factory. I stayed there maybe a month. I was transferred to Dachau for a few weeks, and from Dachau I was transferred to Buchenwald. On January 15, 1945, I was transferred to Ohrdruf, a sub-camp of Buchenwald.

This was the worst camp I had been in since the first one, where we had slept in the barn. We were building a communications center for Germany. I found out later that Hitler was afraid Berlin would be bombed (which it was) so he wanted to move the Nazis' communications center up into the mountains. This was the most horrible camp I was ever in.

We were dynamiting holes into the mountains, and we didn't know what was going to happen any minute. We had no warning, no helmets, no nothing. We used to bring home kids without arms or legs. It was horrible. As soon as people died, another transport would come in. It was like a conveyor belt. I stayed there until March 31 of 1945.

From about the middle of March, we were hearing sounds of artillery, and reconnaissance planes were flying over the perimeter of the camp. The Germans shot down two American airplanes. They killed two men in one plane and they killed one man in the other plane and captured one. Instead of sending him to a POW camp as the Geneva Convention requires, they put him in our camp.

I remember that young fellow. He was a nice-looking kid. He still had his dog tags on. And he went to work, just like anybody else.

On March 31, the camp was evacuated at a very fast tempo. We could hear the artillery maybe five miles away. We lined up and we marched. We didn't know where we were going. East, west, north, south, it didn't make any difference. The guards were getting nervous. *Schnell! Schnell! Schnell! Schnell!*

Some people couldn't keep up. The Germans were shooting them and kicking them to the side of the road. There was a Russian POW among the prisoners who I think saved my life. He said, "If we don't run away now, they're going to kill us."

There were four of us—me, the POW, whose name was Sasha, a Jewish boy from Holland named Hans and a Jewish boy from Warsaw. I can't recall his name. Sasha told us to take off our shoes and drop them as we walked, because they had wooden soles and would make too much noise. Then we dropped our blankets and then our little eating cup. This was all our possessions.

We worked our way up to the front row of our group. From there we could see where the guard was. When the guard was away, we slipped into the woods beside the road. We stayed there until the thousands of prisoners had gone by.

Sasha thought we should go back to the camp, since the artillery sounds were coming from that direction. It took us six or seven hours to walk there through the woods. The shooting was very close, and we were afraid to go into the camp. We knew about an air-raid shelter on the highway and decided to go there. We were barefooted. No food, no water, no nothing. We didn't have grass even to bite. We stayed there four days.

On April 4, 1945, we looked through the little window and saw tanks on the highway. We didn't know what army it was, but we could tell it wasn't the Germans, so we decided to go out. The soldiers pointed guns at us. We sat down and didn't do anything. We started talking in Polish, Russian, Dutch, German, and these soldiers don't understand a word of any of them. They were GIs. They were Americans.

Finally they called over a medic who apparently was from a Czech family. He had a dialect that was similar to Polish. We started telling him who we are. He told the soldiers to put their guns away. Finally these GIs go to the trucks and bring out champagne and wines and K-rations and gave them to us. We were so hungry we ate too much and we threw it all up.

A captain put us in a big Jeep and we showed him where the camp was. There were piles of people lying on the railroad sidings. Their bodies were disintegrating. We looked in the barracks. There were more bodies there. Hundreds of people. It was a massacre. And right on top of one of the piles was the American soldier, the pilot who had been shot down.

We cleaned up one of the barracks and stayed there until the middle of April 1945. On April 12, General Eisenhower, General Patton, and General Bradley came to visit the camp. A few days later, we left.

But where should I go? I didn't know. I asked somebody where the Americans had settled, and I and three or four other guys decided to go there, to a little town called Gotha, about seven miles from the camp.

As we came to the outskirts of Gotha, we were arrested by the American MPs. They took us to a camp in the town. Every nationality was there. A couple of days later, I sneaked out of the camp and went to the city and went into the lobby of a bank.

I saw an American soldier, about six-foot-three or six-foot-five, probably over 200 pounds. I weighed only seventy-five pounds at the time. You could tell I came from a concentration camp. I said to the soldier, in German, "I want to work." And he answered me in Jewish, "You want to work?"

I thought I was going to die. I said, "Are you Jewish?" He said, "Yes, I'm Jewish. My name is Albert Schwartz, and I'm from the Bronx, New York." I told him who I was and where I had been, and he got me a job working in the kitchen for the Army. They fixed up a little room for me with a GI cot and a blanket. They gave me an Eisenhower jacket and a pair of Army shoes and a hat.

Al Schwartz introduced me to a Jewish lieutenant name Ben Kaplan. He took a liking to me, and everything went beautiful. On June 1, 1945, there was an agreement that the Russians would take over the east and the Americans would go west. I was in East Germany at Gotha. A soldier named Emmanuel Rostow from Chicago told me the Americans were leaving at three o'clock the next morning. "If you want to go with us," he said, "you're welcome." I said, "Who's coming?" He told me the Russians were coming.

He sneaked me onto a truck, and we drove for many, many hours. We went to Wetzlar, Germany. Then Rostow told me to go give the commanding officer some excuse for being where I was, some story how I got there. I told him I came on a bicycle. He gave me a funny look, but didn't question anything.

In September 1945, the Army started coming back to the United States. Al Schwartz had a bride waiting in New York, ready to get married. I stayed with Ben Kaplan, who had an important job working with transportation and supplies for displaced persons in the Western Zone of Germany. He made me a big shot. He put me in charge of a warehouse. I was making $200 a month and was allowed to send $100 of it to the United States. I sent it to Al Schwartz, and he opened a bank account for me. So I accumulated some money. I worked there until 1948.

I didn't want to go back to Poland. I was a second-class citizen there. They had taken away my family. I didn't know where they were. Ben Kaplan helped me get my papers to go to the United States. Al Schwartz offered to let me live with him and his new bride in their apartment, which was one bedroom, a small living room, and a little kitchen.

Then right before I was supposed to leave, I got sick with jaundice. The transport left without me. I wound up in a hospital for a month. Luckily, Ben Kaplan had a lot of pull. A few months later, I came to the United States. October 31, 1948. And who met me at the boat in Manhattan? Al Schwartz, his new bride, his father, his mother, his brothers, his sisters, the whole family.

I had a little cot in the living room of their very small apartment. Al took me to the barbershop for a haircut. Then, I'll never forget it, he took me to the Fordham Road Savings & Loan bank, and he gave me my book with my money listed in it. I had almost $7,000. Al was as poor as a church mouse. He could have taken all my money, but here it all was. Every penny. And we became friends for life. He died a few years ago. His widow still lives in the same apartment I came to in 1948.

In November of '48 I was invited to an engagement party. I was introduced to an old gentleman named Morris Laufer, who was from Dallas. He wore a three-piece suit and a gold watch and chain. He asked me where I was from. I said, "Lodz." He said, "I'm from Lodz, too. You must be a relative." He had come to Dallas many years before. I really needed a relative. Believe me, I really needed a relative.

But we couldn't connect. When he left, he said, "Leo, if you don't like New York, I can get you a job in Dallas." I said to him, "To be honest, I don't like New York. I'm just a little frog in a big pond." I had a good job at the warehouse. I had moved out of the Schwartz apartment. I learned how to use the subway. I went to school at night. It was lovely. But New York was too big for me. I couldn't adjust.

About two weeks later, Morris Laufer called me. "Leo," he said, "I talked to Charlie Kupfer. He has a dry-goods store on Elm Street called Rude's. He will call you. He wants to know if you speak good English."

Mr. Kupfer offered me a job. I took the train from Grand Central Station and came to Dallas three days later. I got a room at the Dallas Hotel near the railroad station. I took a nap and shaved and made myself presentable and went to see my new boss.

He was asleep in the back of the store. When I introduced myself, he said, "It's two o'clock in the afternoon. I know you came in at seven o'clock this morning. Where have you been?" I told him I hadn't slept in thirty-six hours and had taken a nap. He said, "OK."

I rented a room in South Dallas from a plumber named Mr. Marx. I worked at Rude's until March of '49. One day I was standing out in front of the store and a gentleman walked by me by the name of Ike Zesner. I had met him before. He was a big name in the Jewish community. He had a chain of shoe stores.

He said, "Leo, you are too aggressive to work for a little outfit like this. Can you leave the store for a minute?" Next door was a five-and-ten-cent store. We went to the lunch counter there and talked. He said, "Leo, I have a friend named Louis Wolens. He has a chain of stores in Corsicana. I think you would fit in perfectly. Let me see if he can give you a job. You have no future where you are."

The next Sunday, Mr. Zesner picked me up and we drove to Corsicana. I met Louis Wolens. He and his brothers owned a chain all over East Texas called K. Wolens. About twenty-nine stores at the time. He liked me. He said, "I want you. How soon can you get away?"

Monday, I gave Mr. Kupfer a week's notice. He said, "You can go right now." He paid me, and that was it. I called Mr. Wolens, and he sent somebody to pick me up. I worked in stores in Gladewater and Longview and Marshall, all around. Then to a big store in Corpus Christi.

In 1950 I married Shirley Somer. She was born in Dallas. Even her mother was born right in Dallas. Her father came from Europe at the turn of the century.

Then, in 1953, I opened up a store in Cleburne and managed it. Mr. Wolens watched me like a hawk. Finally, he said, "Leo, I want you in the main office. I want to train you to be a buyer."

I wound up working for this company for thirty-one years. By the time I left, we had sixty-nine stores and I was vice president of the company. In 1981, we sold out the company.

In 1983 I went back to Poland for the first time. To be honest, I didn't really want to go back to a country where I had been a second-class citizen, but I had four reasons: I wanted to find the grave of my brother who died in 1938, and I found it. I wanted to find the Catholic woman who helped me smuggle food into the ghetto and reminisce with her, and I did. I wanted to show my wife and my daughter how we lived, ten people in two rooms, and I found the house and showed them.

And I wanted to find the barn where I was first incarcerated. Through the years, I had begun thinking it was a fantasy, maybe it didn't happen, maybe it wasn't true. But, sure enough, I found it. And I found a woman who remembered some Jews sleeping there.

The second time I went to Poland, in 1987, I wanted to find out what happened to my father, my mother, my brother, and my four sisters. Somebody tipped me off about Julian Baranowski, a Catholic who wrote a book about the Lodz ghetto. He was in charge of the archives. He took me there. There were millions of documents and pictures strewn all over the place. I found the seven documents about the members of my family. Mr. Baranowski let me have them.

When I got back to the hotel and really looked at them, I almost had a heart attack. Those documents told me everything about my family—their ages, dates of birth, everything. But there was something I didn't understand. All the documents have the date January 18, 1942, and then the words "Transport III." What did this mean? Why had they taken away my whole family at the same time? Usually, the Nazis would take away the old people first, and then the sick, those that couldn't work. They didn't take entire families together.

Mr. Baranowski gave me the answer. Transport III was the third group of people to be taken from the Lodz ghetto. They were taken to a place called Chelmo, about fifteen miles from Lodz, where 385,000 Jews were gassed. There was no camp there. The people were held in the mill, in the Catholic church, and in a castle. They undressed the people and put them into trucks, and the exhaust from the trucks was piped into the back. While they were driving, the gas killed the people. They cremated the bodies and ground up their bones in a mill.

Why did they select my whole family for this? I learned that they designated people they considered "unsocial." People who had been tried for various offenses and their families. They took my whole family because I had been arrested by the Gestapo for smuggling food. If it hadn't been for me, maybe they would have taken them one or two at a time, and maybe one or two of them would have survived. That is a guilt I have to bear.

I went to Chelmo. The mill and the castle were ruined. The Catholic church had been remodeled. It was beautiful. In the woods, there was a bare place cleared for several miles. Nothing grows there. It's just sand. This was the grave of the Jews.

After that trip, I felt I had closure to an extent. I knew what had happened. Maybe some days pass when I don't think about these things, when I'm with my grandkids or something. But most of the time it's very hard. How could human beings do these things? I will never understand it. I put a marble memorial plaque for my family in the Holocaust Center here in Dallas and another in Jerusalem. That's all I can do.

But the good part is, I came to this country in 1948 with two suitcases, with no family whatsoever, and I pulled myself up. I've got four beautiful daughters. All of them graduated from college and graduate school. I've got four sons-in-law that I can call sons, and ten lovely grandchildren. I am blessed. God has been good to me. In my case, Hitler didn't win.

Captain James L. Bell has been a firefighter in Plano for over thirty years.
Courtesy *The Dallas Morning News*, Andy Scott, photographer.

James Bell

Captain James Bell, fifty-nine, has been a firefighter in Plano, Texas, since 1962, first as a volunteer and later as a professional. He says he has more seniority than any other current employee of the city of Plano.

Fire Station 6 at Legacy and Alma is in the area where I was born. My twin brother, Bob, and I were born at home on the farm there. It wasn't far out of Plano even then, but it was awfully muddy. Everything was mud. There were some gravel roads, but out where we lived, that was all mud. It was tough getting in and out of there. It was old black mud, and you can't hardly go in that stuff.

My dad was born in 1918 at home right in that same area. My family came here from Kentucky, but I can't remember when. A lot of my family is buried at Rowlett Cemetery.

This was a cotton-farming area. There was a lot of cotton. My uncle was farming the land where Middlekoff Ford and Ewing Buick are now. I worked with him a lot out there. I loved farming. I didn't like to chop cotton, but I liked to farm.

Plano has around 150,000 people now. Back then, about 1958, it had maybe 1,200 people, maybe not that many. There were three red lights, and you couldn't get through town hardly without stopping for all three of them. They were only a block apart, on 14th, 15th, and 16th, and no matter what speed you drove, you hit all of them on red.

My twin, Bob Bell, and I went all through school in the same building, which is the Cox Administration Building now. My dad graduated there, too. Bob is the constable in this precinct here in Plano and has been since 1976.

When we were still kids, we moved from the farm into town. A big box factory burned behind the old cotton gin back in 1949. We lived close to there, and that fire kind of piqued our dad. The next thing we knew, he was in the Fire Department. He was a fireman from '49 until '62.

It was a volunteer department then. But we always had a station attendant who lived with his wife and family at the top of the fire station. For many, many years. I don't even know when that started. That stopped in 1960, when they hired the first guy to work twenty-four hours. He and another guy kind of split it up.

The fire marshal was kind of a paid man, too. I'm not sure just how that worked. Anyway, they started hiring paid men in '60. They were hiring out of the volunteers. Anybody who was willing to go to work for that kind of money, they let them.

My brother and I went to a lot of fires with my dad when we were kids. We never knew what the fire was unless we could see the smoke. The station attendant would blow the siren that was on top of the building and would put a blackboard out in front of the station and write the address or directions to the fire, and the volunteers had to drive by the station to find out where to go. Later on, they put the siren up on the water tower, which was behind the station, so you could hear it farther away.

Bob and I started going to fires with our dad when we were about nine, and I got in the volunteers in 1962. I was working at the Jones-Blair Paint Co. I already wanted to come to work as a regular fireman, but it was '69 before I managed to. The department was still part volunteer until '72.

By '69 the town was beginning to grow some, and people was dropping out of the department. They didn't like chasing the fire trucks through so much traffic. And it was tough. We didn't realize that traffic wasn't anything compared to what it was going to be. So we decided we would just do away with the volunteer fire department.

I went to work as a paid firefighter February 1 of '69. I never was interested in moving up in rank. I always liked being on shift. I didn't want to get off that.

Then in 1986, I fell at a fire and broke a kneecap. I had to rehab for three months or so. They had an opening for a captain to run the inspection program, so after awhile I decided to see about doing that. I always liked inspections anyway.

I did that until '91, then they gave that to the fire marshal's office, which is where it probably ought to have been anyway. So I went to work where I am now, in support services. I take care of the buildings and all the equipment that we use and all the vehicles. I have to get them serviced and to the shop. And all the clothes. It's a big job, and there's just three of us to do it.

Plano has ten fire stations and more than 250 personnel now. When I joined it, I was the ninth man in. They still had about twenty-five volunteers then. And the nine of us worked as volunteers, too, when we weren't on duty. In April of '69, they hired six more firemen. In October, they hired six more. All but one of them had been in the volunteers.

Eventually a lot of them didn't work out or they didn't stay. A lot of times, when you're doing something for fun, it doesn't work out when it turns out to be your job.

We had some guys who didn't particularly like going in burning houses. When it's your job, it's a lot different than it is when you're playing. When you're playing, you don't have to go in if you don't want to.

That doesn't seem like it would be a big thing. But when you go in a burning house and you can't see anything, if you start thinking about yourself, you're not going to stay. You're looking for people. A lot of times we know there's nobody in a burning building, but a lot of times we don't. So we have to look. We lost quite a few men who didn't want to do that. It turned out not to be their thing, you know.

I was twenty-one when I became a volunteer. You had to be

twenty-one. I was working at the Jones-Blair Paint Co. in Dallas. I liked it there. I never worked anywhere I didn't like. I had to run thinner through the paint machines to clean them up every evening. That thinner got hot in the machines and put out a steam that would just knock you out.

A lot of evenings, I was so whacked out on fumes that I would have to lie down. I would tell my wife, "I've just got to get out of that place someday." Because I would get out of my car at home drunk from the fumes. So I quit and went to work for the Fire Department.

I thought they had stopped my pay when I got my first check. My gosh. I think I was bringing home like $140 a week at Jones-Blair. And my first check at the Fire Department was $168 for half the month.

So I stayed down at Jones-Blair two years part time. I worked part time at stores and service stations sometimes, too. I always liked my jobs.

I worked part time for a surveying company here in Plano for ten years in the late '70s and the '80s. There was a lot of surveying going on in those days. There was a lot of paper-trading going around. People were selling the land to each other over and over again every month or so to drive up the price. That's when all that savings-and-loan stuff was going on. I never could figure out what was going on really.

Every time a piece of land sold, it had to be surveyed. We surveyed some of that land so often we nearly wore it out. It was hot in the summer and cold in the winter, but there were a lot of good times of the year, too. I enjoyed being out.

Firefighting has changed a lot since I started. We used to just show up and go in a burning house and stay in there till it's out. Now we go in and stay until our air bottle runs out, then you've got to go to rehab.

They say a bottle is supposed to last forty-five minutes, maybe an hour. But you go in there, and you're breathing like a racehorse, and they last twenty, maybe twenty-five minutes. Some people still like to come out, change their bottle and go back in. But a lot of these young guys are ready to get out and watch things happen after one bottle.

We didn't have any air bottles when I first came to work here. We had some canister mask things. They were real restrictive. You couldn't hardly breathe through them. It was easier to breathe without them, so we would take them off.

Also, they set up command posts now, and have one person in charge of the scene. That's good, because you know where everybody's at and what everybody's doing. Everybody's accounted for. If we come out of a burning building and one guy's still in there, we know it and can go in and get him.

That's a big improvement over the old days.

Ann Cushing Gantz, pictured in her studio, is a well-known Dallas artist and art teacher. Courtesy *The Dallas Morning News*, Kim Ritzenthaler, photographer.

Ann Cushing Gantz

"The current thought is, if you are accessible, you're no good. Establishment art today has to be 'difficult' or 'upsetting' or 'natural.' Especially 'difficult.'"—Ann Cushing Gantz

In high school, I won a little award here, a little ribbon there. Back then, you didn't have an art teacher on every corner. I wanted to go to an art academy, but my parents said no, you have to go to college. And I had another argument with my parents: They wanted me to go to a girls' school and I wanted to go to a wild school.

I got sent to Newcomb College in New Orleans, which is part of Tulane. Before it became part of Tulane, it was Sophie Harriet Newcomb College for Young White Unmarried Gentlewomen. That was its official name. It was a fun place to go. I had wonderful teachers.

When I graduated, in 1955, my family moved from Memphis back to Dallas, where I had been born. One of my art history professors told me to look up a man he knew in Dallas called Everett Rassiga who owned the Black Tulip Gallery. I did, and he said, "We'll give you a show." Everett was a real interesting character and a very good salesman.

The Black Tulip is where I met my Everett, my husband, who was an aeronautical engineer. He was a silent partner in the gallery. So I graduated from Newcomb in May, moved to Dallas in July and had a major one-man show in October. Which, of course, was too early because I had to use mostly the work I had done in school and during that summer.

I was just lucky, lucky, lucky. I had a little angel flying over my head. There are so many people now who knock on gallery doors forever and never get in.

I met a woman named Rose Rolnick, whose husband owned a hat factory. She said she wanted to study painting with me. I said, "I don't teach." She said, "Well, just come to my house and I'll have a few friends over and we'll give it a try." I loved it. I thought it was great.

This was in early 1956. The Dallas Museum of Fine Art, which was in Fair Park at that time, had a program called Artists in Action. And the director of the museum, Jerry Bywaters, asked me to do woodcuts for Artists in Action, which I did.

I met a woman there named Ruth Tears, who was a painter and was starting to teach, so we decided to share a studio. We rented space in an old barn on North Central Expressway, so we called it The Barn. It was rickety. She had classes three days a week and I had classes three days a week.

It worked out great. But the owner finally sold the land and The Barn was torn down. They just put a rope around it and pulled it down with a pickup truck.

One of my students was Irving Bock, who had an air-conditioning company. I had another student named Fran Newman. They offered to find me another studio. Then they said no, let's open a gallery. By this time it was 1960. We called it Cushing Galleries. Mr. Bock put up half the money and Fran Newman put up half the money, and I put up my expertise, which was a good deal for me. We were one of the first tenants in the Quadrangle. That lasted thirteen years. It was a great adventure.

The painter who has influenced my own work the most is Robert Rauschenberg. I like the drippity stuff. My students are always asking me, "Teach us how to do the drippity stuff." The French have a word for it. *Eclat dousage*. And then you put a glaze on top. I love the texture. I don't do really abstract paintings, but liking the drippity stuff precludes doing strict realism.

The first thing beginners have to learn is that you're not just born with the gift. People think, "Well, here I am. I'm going to paint a picture and take it home today and frame it tomorrow and everybody's going to say how great I am." When they can't do that, sometimes they think, "Well, I have no talent. I might as well give up."

Those people probably should give up. Talent is an intangible thing, and nobody knows whether he has it until time has gone by. But anyone who has the desire and wants to work can learn to paint, and paint well. Whether they turn out to be Rembrandt or not is where the talent comes in. The most important thing to learn is that you have to work. And think.

There's something very sensual about putting the paint on the canvas and manipulating it and making it do what you want it to do. Those few times when it really does what you want it to do, nothing is more exciting.

You also have to get over the idea that you have to have a style right away. People come into a class thinking, "I want to paint like Renoir. I want to paint like Monet." If you try to do that, then the very, very best you can be is a pretty good copy of Renoir or Monet.

A better goal is to say something of your own. You find out what that is by experimenting. It's surprising how many students do come up with something unique to themselves, that's not a carbon copy of somebody else's style.

Most of my students do art as a hobby, but I've had some who have gone on to make careers. I can't say I've had Andrew Wyeth, but quite a few have been good enough to make a living painting. I've had several who teach now.

The art scene in Dallas has changed wildly since I've been teaching here. Today it's kind of goofy. It's goofy in the rest of the country, too. I know one lady who was a good artist who kept trying to get NEA grants and trying to get into shows and never got anywhere. So she got a bunch of old wood boxes and hammered nails in them, and then hung little pieces of doll anatomy on the nails. A leg here, a head there, an arm here.

And she got a big grant from the NEA with that. She did it almost as a joke, you know. But she began to believe her own boxes. She gave me a big speech about how symbolic and deep and meaningful they are. So now she just does boxes, and she's in a lot of shows, hanging little doll parts.

There were only three galleries in Dallas when I started. Now there are about sixty. They've divided themselves into two equal camps: those that show nothing but corny stuff, like paintings of bluebonnets and sweet little children kissing dogs; and those that show the wood boxes with the nails and the arms hanging on them, trying to be different for difference's sake.

The current thought is, if you are accessible, you're no good. Establishment art today has to be "difficult" or "upsetting" or "natural." Especially "difficult." There's a lot of hot air that goes with it.

I don't want to do that kind of thing. It doesn't take any skill. But that's part of the contemporary art ethic: We don't want skill. Skill is considered artifice. Today your work is supposed to look primitive or childlike or cartoony. The worse it is, the better it is.

I'm turning into a curmudgeon.

I remember when I first came to Dallas, I was doing more abstract things than I do now. Kind of cubistic. And there were these old guys who did ducks flying over the water. I thought they were so old-fashioned and corny. Now people coming out of school look at me and think I'm old-fashioned and corny. Which is not a good thought.

Two-year-old Makenna Schulte gets a boost from master puppeteer John Hardman to help her get acquainted with one of his marionettes. Courtesy *The Dallas Morning News*, Natalie Caudill, photographer.

John Hardman

John Hardman, sixty-five, grew up in Wichita Falls, where, he says, there was nothing to do. But he discovered puppets there, and they've been his livelihood ever since.

My dad got me out of school once, and we went down to watch the circus unload. Ringling Bros. had come to town. We watched them unload the trains and set up, and then we went to the evening performance. I was about seven.

We got there a little early. Ringling Bros. had a sideshow, and there was a guy there doing Punch and Judy with hand puppets. I had never seen anything like it. I figured there must be nine people back there doing this thing. Then this guy walks out alone and takes a bow. I thought, "How in the world can one guy do all that?" That's all I talked about for a while.

That Christmas, my dad got me a set of commercially made marionettes from a company called Hazelle Marionettes out of Kansas City. I woke up to find all these Little Red Riding Hood marionettes. Red Riding Hood, the wolf, grandma, the whole thing. I didn't know anything about marionettes. I played with them for a while and then put them away.

When I was about nine years old, a group of marionette performers came to my school. This was in the '40s, when performing groups traveled a school circuit and put on a show during assembly. I had never seen marionettes really work. I came unglued. Gollee! I didn't know they would do that! And I had some at home!

I immediately turned our garage into a puppet theater. We lived across the street from a Baptist church, and they had a tabernacle out back. It was just a roof and some wooden benches. I confiscated some of those benches and pulled them into the garage. I did Little Red Riding Hood for the neighborhood kids and charged them a nickel.

I couldn't figure out why they didn't come the next week. Then I realized, once you've seen a show, you've seen it. So I started going to the library and reading all the books I could find about puppetry. There weren't many.

One day a magician came to my school. I got thoroughly involved in magic. There was plenty of literature on that. I had a little suitcase about fifteen inches square. On one side I wrote: "John Hardman Puppets," and on the other side I wrote: "John Hardman Magician." Whichever I was doing, that was the side that faced out.

I was invited to the Wichita Falls Public Library to do a marionette show, to do Little Red Riding Hood. It was my first real show. I thought, "Man, this is big-time. This is my big opportunity."

My show was supposed to be on a Saturday morning. I was not really prepared. I put on probably the worst show they had seen in their existence. Now, not only was I not invited back, they didn't even speak to me after the show. This taught me a valuable lesson about rehearsals.

I messed around with magic and puppets all through high school, got into the music program, learned music, played in the band. I talked the band director into producing a variety show instead of a spring concert, and talked him into letting it be student-directed.

So my junior and senior years, 1952 and '53, I produced that show and it was a great hit. In fact, they still do it.

In the summers of '52 and '53, I begged a radio station to let me work for free. KFDX in Wichita Falls, "high atop the City National Bank Building." I wanted to learn the business. So they said, "OK, you can file records." So I sat up there all summer, filing records.

Then they let me do other things, too. I did the same thing the following summer. I got to learn the business pretty well. I even got to pull an announce shift on Sunday.

I graduated from high school in '53 and that summer they opened the first TV station in Wichita Falls. Channel 3. I moved over there. During my time in college at Midwestern University, I worked there. I started as a floor man and worked my way up to cameraman and eventually director. I was even on air for a while, doing clown magic stuff.

I worked my way through college that way. During my junior year, the Marriott Hotel here in Dallas—the old one on Stemmons that doesn't exist anymore—spread the word that they were looking for entertainers. They wanted to cater to families on the weekends. I applied as a magician and got a job and made some pretty good money that year.

I finished college. All my buddies were being drafted into the occupation army in Korea, and I didn't want to do that, so I joined the Marine Corps and spent the next three years in Southern California.

I came back to Dallas in 1960 and was doing shows on McKinney Avenue, which was kind of a coffeehouse row back then. I was working at the Eighth Day, which was a little cabaret theater on one side and a bar on the other side.

They hired three of us to do a funny little cabaret show, a spoof called *How Cleopatra Made Her Mark*. The characters were Cleopatra, Marc Antony, and a puppet character named Argyle Asp. A very campy show. There was a girl in it named Patty Reed. Patty Garrett was her stage name. She was just out of Baylor. We got married.

That show ran for a long, long time. I was working at Channel 4, and at night I would go to the Eighth Day and do the show.

Suddenly, Six Flags opened. They called me and said, "We understand you do Punch and Judy." I told them I did. They said they were going to build a Punch and Judy wagon for one of their sections and asked me to come talk to them.

I auditioned and they hired me for more money than I was making at the TV station. So I turned my hobby into a profession, and off I went.

I worked for Six Flags for twenty-some-odd years. I started with Punch and Judy, doing twenty-two shows a day. The muscles in my arms were so tired that after about two weeks I couldn't hold anything, not even a cup of coffee. I was working with Ace bandages wrapped around my arms. I finally got used to it, but it was so boring, the same show twenty-two times a day.

Just to cut the boredom, I brought Argyle Asp out to the park. Between shows, he would just come out and talk to people. Well, the owner of Six Flags, Angus Wynne, saw it one day and said, "Cut out that Punch and Judy crap. We want Argyle." I changed his name to Argyle Snake. I built a whole act around him and did him at Six Flags.

In 1967, Rainbo Bakeries gave me a call and said, "We'd like to have Argyle at HemisFair in San Antonio." I spent a year traveling all the major towns in Texas, using Argyle to promote HemisFair and Rainbo Bakeries. Then I worked HemisFair itself.

That's where I met Sid and Marty Krofft. They had two big puppet shows there. One they had had at the New York World's Fair. They had just made a deal with Six Flags to build puppet theaters at all their parks. Sid and Marty told me if I wanted a job, come on by. I didn't at the time. I was too involved with Argyle.

During my time at Channel 4, I had met Mark Wilson, the magician. He was doing a show on Channel 4 called Mark Wilson's Magic Circus, sponsored by Frito-Lay. I did some clown work for him. About the time I finished HemisFair, Mark got a CBS show called *The Magic Land of Alakazam*. It was on CBS for about six seasons. He called me to come out to California and work with him.

I worked with Mark for five or six years. I also worked for Sid and Marty Krofft and was learning how to produce a large marionette show. All their shows at the Six Flags parks involved about ten puppeteers and 200 to 300 marionettes.

Patty and I decided to move back to Dallas. So Sid and Marty said I could be the lead puppeteer at the Arlington Six Flags. I started doing Argyle Snake again. Eventually I took over the puppet theater at Six Flags and produced my first big show in '78.

In 1979, NorthPark said, "We need something out here for Christmas." So I devised a one-man Scrooge puppet show, based on my old Argyle Snake routine. Scrooge has been going ever since. Twenty years now.

Six Flags grew and grew and grew. They asked me to produce shows everywhere. There was a time when we were producing thirty-five shows for Six Flags in one year, all over the system. I had about 160 employees and hated it.

They bought Magic Mountain in California, and we moved out there again. They built a theater for me there. It was too big. The thing would seat 1,000 people. Puppets were too small for it. But it ran for three years.

Then in the early '80s, Warner Bros. bought Six Flags and the fun went out of it. So Patty and I said, "Let's move back to Texas where our friends are." So back to Dallas. And here I am. I was tired. Burned out. My wife teaches theater arts at Woodrow Wilson High School, so I took some time off, did some free-lance work.

Originally, Le Theatre de Marionette was in Arlington, opened by one of my ex-employees, John Hopkins, in '93. It got so successful that the landlord tripled his rent. So I talked to NorthPark about bringing it here. I bought it from John in '97 and I've been running it since. I do this and a show at the State Fair every year, and that's all I want to do now.

And I'm told I'll be doing Scrooge until they carry me away in a box. The mall says if they didn't have Scrooge at Christmas, people would tear the place down.

It's difficult for puppets to compete with TV and video games in this day and age. But puppets are a novelty to kids. It's new to them. I get comments from moms, saying this was their child's first theater experience. Since it's geared to children, they feel comfortable with it. Kids are fascinated with the marionettes. They want to see how everything works. To them, it's a live cartoon.

I don't perform much anymore. My biggest joy now is writing the shows. I love puns. I throw in as many puns as I can get away with without being stoned to death.

We do mostly fairy tales. The most popular ones are *Pinocchio* and *Hansel and Gretel*. We do our version of *The Wizard of Oz*. That's pretty popular. In the summer, the most popular show is *The Little Mermaid*. We do *Cinderella*, but it's not popular with boys. We do it in the summer when the boys are out playing baseball and the girls want to be inside where it's cool.

Patty and I have raised four kids and put them all through college with puppets. Now I'm performing for my grandchildren. What could be better than that?

Abel Reyna, principal of Arcadia Park summer school, is shown with one of the slides he once used to teach Texas history in San Antonio. Courtesy *The Dallas Morning News*, David Leeson, photographer.

Abel Reyna

Abel Reyna, fifty-seven, grew up in Lyford,
Texas, and taught school in San Antonio for
many years. He's now the principal of Lorenzo de
Zavala Elementary School in Dallas.

I started working on my Texas history project in 1972. I was an elementary schoolteacher. I had just gone to work for the Edgewood Independent School District in San Antonio, where I would work for twenty-two years.

I had been hired as a "cultural advocate," a rather dubious role. Nobody knew what I was supposed to do. I figured I had to be some kind of authority on history. So history was something I just picked up.

My main interest is in the Hispanics who were involved in the early history of Texas. Texas for sure has a very, very Hispanic flavor to it. Especially San Antonio. And its dramatic history is what makes San Antonio what it is.

Every time I go to San Antonio, I envision what it was in the beginning. La Villita was where the rich elite—the Canary Islanders—lived. La Villita was the Highland Park of San Antonio at that time. And across town was what they now call San Pedro Creek, where the poor people lived.

One of the most recognized buildings in the world is the Alamo. Nobody goes to San Antonio who doesn't also see the Alamo. I know the history of the Alamo. I know it was moved three times to where it is today. They moved not the building but the name.

I developed a fascination for people like Gregorio Esparza, who died defending the Alamo, and Juan Seguin. Seguin was a captain in the army of the Republic of Texas. He was one of the messengers that Travis sent out of the Alamo to recruit volunteers, so he wasn't at the Alamo when it fell. There was another messenger named Blas Herrera. Seguin fought at San Jacinto, too.

Francisco Ruiz was one of the signers of the Texas Declaration of Independence. And he was one of Texas' first public school-teachers. I dug out information about him when I taught at a school in San Antonio that bore his name: Jose Francisco Ruiz Elementary School.

In 1967 my class from Ruiz Elementary and I went down to the Bexar County Archives and talked to Richard Santos, who is the foremost archivist there. He took us into the depths of the courthouse where they keep the archives. They don't let just any Tom, Dick, and Harry go down there, you know. You've got to be pretty serious about what you're doing.

It was while I was doing my research on Francisco Ruiz that I found out about the Hispanic guys inside the Alamo. There were twelve or thirteen Hispanics in there.

I found out about Gregorio Esparza. He was a cannoneer for the Texans. His brother, Francisco, was in Santa Anna's army, under the command of Martin Perfecto Cos, Santa Anna's brother-in-law.

Gregorio Esparza was the only Alamo defender who had a Christian burial. His brother Francisco asked Santa Anna for his body, and Santa Anna gave it to him. I have a copy of an affidavit signed by Francisco shortly before he died. He says his brother was, in fact, inside the Alamo.

Enrique Esparza, the son of Gregorio, witnessed the arrival of General Antonio Lopez de Santa Anna in Main Plaza, which was in front of San Fernando Cathedral at the time. You could see the Alamo from the cathedral then, because the land between them was barren in those days.

I dug up a lot of information and wrote a script and paid a guy money to draw me eighteen slides about the death of Gregorio Esparza. I gave him five bucks an hour to just sit and draw. And I went down to the Mexican TV station in San Antonio and they let me borrow some sound effects.

At night I would sit down with two or three tape recorders and do the voice, and then go back and put the voice with the sound effects. Cannons, rifle shots, horses running away, screams and yells and shouts. What I envisioned in my own head to have been the scene at the Alamo.

I put together a slide show and showed it at schools and different groups. I still have the script, but I don't know what happened to the sound effects. And it's hard to find a projector to show the slides now. The technology is Stone Age.

I would like to revive the show somehow and find a way to put it to use. Make presentations, you know. I'm not in it for money, but I would like to get credit for having done what I've done. So other people could appreciate Texas history from a point of view they may not know about. How Hispanics were tied into it. Because the Texas Revolution was not a war between the gringos and the Mexicans. It was about the politics of the time.

Of course, Hispanics weren't called Hispanics then. When I went to school, I was Latin American. We were called Latins. I refused to identify with that. I'm not Latin.

The Hispanic contribution to Texas history has been ignored for a long time. Whenever I look at a textbook, I look for certain names. If they're not there, I don't think the book is worth a hoot. If it doesn't have Francisco Ruiz, if it doesn't have Juan Seguin, if it doesn't have Antonio Navarro, if it doesn't have Lorenzo de Zavala, it's just not worth a hoot. It was written from a one-sided view.

You can't rely too much on books. You have to teach the kids some of the things that aren't in books. We have to research our own information. We have to dig around like a pig in the forest.

I think the prejudice against Hispanics started with the battle cry: "Remember the Alamo!" But Pancho Villa had a lot to do with it, too. Except for the English who tried to burn Washington in the

War of 1812, nobody but Pancho Villa has ever dared attack the continental United States. He took an army into the little town of Columbus, New Mexico.

Yeah, there were a lot of border raids, but none like Pancho Villa's invasion. Juan Cortina, the bandit, based himself out of Brownsville. His guys went left and right and did a lot of things. That did a lot to create more hatred than was there already.

And Americo Paredes, the foremost historian at the University of Texas, who died recently, wrote a book about the legend of the border bandit Gregorio Cortez. It's called *With His Pistol in His Hand*. It's a classic. I used to have a slide show about that guy, too. He stood up to the Texas Rangers.

I've got stuff on another guy named Gus Garcia. You know who he was? He was one of the early civil rights lawyers from San Antonio. In the 1950s or '60s he was the first Mexican-American lawyer to argue before the U.S. Supreme Court. I did research on him when I was the "cultural advocate" at that school in San Antonio.

It's changing. There's not as much prejudice as there used to be. I pick up more on it in Dallas than in San Antonio. I've been in Dallas five years, and I've been called a "wetback" about six times. I was never called that in San Antonio.

I don't put up with that crap. I'm like Captain McCrae in *Lonesome Dove*. He said, "I won't tolerate rudeness in a man." Well, I won't tolerate rudeness from anybody, either. We've got road rage. We've got mall rage. There's a lot of rage in Dallas.

My history is not as keen as it used to be. I used to have a lot of books on Texas history. I used to loan them out. But every time I loaned one out, hell, it never came back.

So I've lost a lot of books, but I still have some. What I don't have in my books I have in my head. And I know where to go dig up the information if I need to.

Sam Baker is KERA-FM's local host of National Public Radio's Morning Edition show. Courtesy *The Dallas Morning News*, Allison V. Smith, photographer.

Sam Baker

*Sam Baker's official title is assistant director of
news and public affairs at KERA-FM (90.1), the
North Texas public radio station. But early-risers
and commuters know him best as the mellow-
voiced local host of National Public Radio's
Morning Edition, which airs from five to nine
A.M. every weekday. He's forty-one.*

I grew up in Beaumont, Texas, part of the "Golden Triangle" of
Beaumont, Port Arthur, and Orange. Petrochemical heaven or hell,
depending on how you look at it.

My father was a mail carrier. He passed away about a year ago.
My mother still lives there. She worked as a secretary at DuPont
for a long time, and taught school as a substitute. Many people in
my family—a grandfather, a couple of uncles, some cousins—
worked in the refineries. They retired from Mobil, Texaco,
Bethlehem Steel.

My grandfather was a notary public on the side. When he died
a couple of years ago, he was the oldest certified notary public in
Jefferson County. He was ninety-two or ninety-three.

We lived in the South End section of Beaumont, a predominantly
black section, for a good long while. It was right near Mobil Oil. I
didn't know until my grandfather's funeral that they used to call
him "the South End lawyer." Most people there were not affluent
at all, and legal help was expensive. So when people needed some
basic legal question answered, they would call my grandfather.
He wasn't a lawyer, but he was a notary public. They figured that
was the next best thing.

I went on to the University of Houston and majored in journal-
ism. When I came out, I got a job working as a general assign-

ments reporter for KJEC, Channel 4, the NBC affiliate in Port Arthur. So I got to start at home, which was a good thing. I knew my way around.

Port Arthur was regarded as a beginner's market. Nearly all the reporters there were new. Only one or two had a year more experience than I did when I started. That was the situation with most of the newspaper and TV reporters in town. It was a situation I haven't encountered anywhere since. Since there was absolutely nothing to do in Beaumont and Port Arthur, the reporters hung around with each other.

Of course, the thing we had in common was that we all wanted to get out of Beaumont and Port Arthur. The other thing we had in common was that we all were making extremely little money.

I was there three years. I did general-assignments reporting and hosted a weekly public-affairs series called Black Outreach and did a little anchoring for a while. It kept me pretty busy.

Then a job came along at KOTV, the CBS affiliate in Tulsa, Oklahoma. I did TV for three years there, then went to KWGS, the public radio station, which was licensed and located at the University of Tulsa. And I did that for three years.

In television, particularly commercial television, everything is about time or lack of time. The staff is much bigger, the logistics involved in getting a story are much more complicated. You've got to find your story, research your story, find the people you need to talk to, and then you had better be back at the station by two or two-thirty, because the first newscast is on at five. Typically, they want something for five, for six, and for ten. So there's a mad rush for editing bays. You've got maybe two editing bays and six or eight reporters trying to get into them at the same time.

Public broadcasting is a totally different animal. It's much quieter. The pace is slower. But there's less money in it, and you have fewer people.

The biggest change for me was in television you're lucky if you get a minute and a half or a minute and forty-five seconds for a story. So one day at the public radio station, they tell me I've got eight minutes for one story. "Weird Al" Yankovic is shooting a movie in Tulsa. I think the name of it was *UHF*. They want me to do a feature story about it. I'm thinking, "What the heck am I going to do with all that time?" I was used to thinking in condensed terms.

I went out and interviewed "Weird Al" Yankovic and got a couple of side stories about off-duty policemen who were doing security and things like that. And I somehow filled up the eight minutes.

Eventually, I learned I didn't have to be quite as concise as I had been on TV. And, of course, I no longer had pictures to use as a crutch. I had to use sound and my voice to create the pictures in the listener's mind. It was a difficult challenge. It took some getting used to.

I got to Dallas by way of Boston. In 1991, I went to a two-week seminar on public affairs at WGBH in Boston. By that time—as is often the case with reporters—I had started getting that itch to move, which in my case starts between three and five years in a place. I had no problems with where I was at KWGS. I was having a good time there. I was winning awards, I was growing as a reporter.

Still, I had that itch. One of the people I met at the seminar worked here at KERA. We got to talking, and she said, "We have this Morning Edition position opening." She said it was a part-time position, and they were having trouble finding someone to do it. They were thinking of combining it with another part-time position and making it full time.

It so happened that I had been doing Morning Edition in Tulsa for two years. I told her that, and she said, "OK, when I go back to Dallas, I'll mention your name to the news director." I'm thinking, "Yeah, right." But sure enough, a week or two later, the news director, Marla Crockett at that time, called me to arrange an interview. There was going to be a public radio news directors conference in Atlanta in a couple of weeks, so we arranged to meet there.

That was July of '91. By early September, I was here. I've been doing Morning Edition for KERA ever since.

Of all the questions people ask me, the one that comes up most is: "What time do you have to get up in the morning?" I get up about two A.M. I'm here at KERA about four. Usually, I'm on the air just before five. Every ten minutes after that until nine o'clock, I'm alternating with Bob Edwards on the NPR network.

From four to four-fifty A.M., KERA runs the BBC World Report. At four forty-nine, I switch over to NPR for a thirty-second promo they have for Talk of the Nation. Then I come back, do a local break of thirty seconds or so, then switch over to the Marketplace Morning Report. That goes until about four fifty-nine, then I do a local break until five o'clock straight up, then I switch over to Morning Edition.

Then about every ten minutes, I do weather, traffic, promos for programs, underwriter cards, etc., etc. I have to put all that in about two minutes. Then I switch back to Morning Edition. There are hard starts and stops, which means the break begins at nineteen [minutes after the hour], and Bob Edwards resumes at twenty-one.

I have to hit it just right. I must be back for that bright little story Bob Edwards always does at five-thirty. I must hit that. If I don't, I get calls from people. I also can't cover up Frank DeFord on Wednesdays. There was a time when we were running Red Barber, and oh, no, I'd better not touch Red Barber. There are some aspects of Morning Edition that are just sacred, and I can't cover them up.

I say that because in order to run the stories that our local reporters do, or interviews that I do, or run our local commentators like Tom Dodge, we have to cover up something on Morning Edition. There's no time that Morning Edition just stops for the local stations to do their thing.

In between, I'm writing up newscasts and things. I'm not just sitting there waiting for the next break. I'm alone in the booth. It can be difficult. There have been many times when I've been sitting there writing, trying to get a handle on a story, and all of a sudden I hear Bob Edwards say, "The time is ten minutes before the hour," and I have to be back on in a split second. It doesn't matter what I have to go through to do that. The important thing is that the listener can't tell that I had a problem.

I'm on the air from five till nine. I'm also assistant news director in charge of talk shows and commentaries. I also host a weekly public-affairs show, On the Record, on Channels 13 and 2. Plus meetings. So normally I'm here until around eleven-thiry or noon.

Then I go home and drop. Dinner is at two or three in the afternoon. I go to bed about eight. If I were smart, I would go to bed at six, but I refuse. I don't have much of a social life at all, so I at least allow myself to sit up until eight o'clock, when it's dark. I can't even sleep late on weekends. My body clock won't let me.

But you get used to it. You're like a juggler on autopilot. You just do it. If you like solitude, it's wonderful.

'Big Bill' Johnson, the 'Singing Drywall Man,' isn't shy about singing in the back yard or nearly anywhere else. Johnson never really made it to the big time, but he loves his life in Greenville, Texas. Courtesy *The Dallas Morning News*, Mona Reeder, photographer.

Big Bill Johnson

Big Bill Johnson, Greenville's "Singing Drywall Man," has been picking, singing, and writing country songs for more than fifty years and hanging drywall for more than forty. He says he's "older than dirt," but won't say by how much.

When I was a kid, I bought an old Gibson guitar from an Army sergeant for ten bucks and learned how to play that thing. It had a chunk out of it. That's why I got it so cheap. This was in Louisville, Kentucky. I saw Peewee King and Roy Acuff in a country music show there, and I realized that's what I wanted to do for a living. I was sixteen.

Next thing you know, I was playing in clubs. The drunks were driving me nuts. I also started writing my own songs. The first one was called "Your Love, Sweetheart, I'll Never Forget." A company in New York published it. The fourth song I wrote was "As Long as We're Together." Jimmie Logsdon recorded it for Decca Records in 1952.

Jimmie was a friend of Hank Williams, and he told me Hank liked that song. You remember, Hank Williams died on January 1, 1953, so no telling what might have happened if he had lived a little longer.

Shortly after that, I wrote a song called "That's the Way I Like You the Best," and Carl Smith recorded it. I understand it sold around 100,000 copies.

Drywall was my day job. But I was spending more and more time in Nashville, so I moved down there and signed a contract as a writer for one of the publishing companies. I wrote thousands of songs during that time and since then. Way over 100 of them have been recorded.

I've worked with everybody and his brother at one time or another. Willie Nelson. Bill Anderson. Peewee King. Loretta Lynn. Johnny Cash. I lived in Nashville most of the time from the '60s till the early '80s, except for a time I moved out to Arizona, where I thought I was going to do some stuff for the movies. It didn't work out.

I moved to Greenville in 1982 from Nashville. Everything in Nashville was all pop, and I was writing country. I couldn't hardly give a song away. Christine's daughter and grandkids—Christine's my wife—lived in Greenville, and Christine wanted to move here, so we did. It's the best thing that ever happened to me.

I thought, "Well, I've had a pretty good run in music, so I'll just do drywall from now on." I had the mistaken idea that when you left Nashville, that was the end of the world as far as music was concerned. But I found out I was wrong. When I got to Texas, that was really a new beginning for me.

I didn't do any music at all for a couple of years. When I first come here I got a job doing drywall work on those condos that Danny Faulkner was building on the I-30 corridor. That was the best job I ever had. I didn't make a fortune, but it was steady every week, and it was easy.

But Mr. Faulkner got in that financial trouble, and they shut him down. March 1984. I wrote a song about Danny Faulkner. He liked it real well.

I decided to go in business for myself here in Greenville, doing drywall. I put an ad in the paper and hired a guy or two. It went real good. I joined the Homebuilders Association. I never did tell anybody I had been Big Bill Johnson in Nashville and all the songs I had written.

But in 1985, I was over at Bobby Pickle's lumberyard, and he had a guitar and a mandolin in his office there. We got to playing around, and I had the best time. It kind of rekindled the flame. So I would go in there and play music with Bobby every once in a while.

Then on December 31, 1987, my mother passed away. New Year's Eve. When I was a musician, New Year's Eve had always been the biggest night of the year. I always played music somewhere on New Year's Eve and made pretty good money.

My mother's death really hit me hard, even at my age. My father had died a few years earlier. That hurt me, but it didn't hurt me like my mother. I was having a hard time getting over it. I started fooling around with music again to try to help me.

I wrote a song called "Drywall Man." I put that on a cassette with a bunch of other songs of mine. About the same time, Bob Phillips, the Texas Country Reporter on TV, was starting his Texas Country Tours by bus around the state. I called and told him I was a country music entertainer, and he said, "Come on, and bring your guitar."

I wrote a little song about Texas Country Tours, and Bob just loved it. He did a show later, and he had me sing that song all the way through it. I sang it over and over, and that got me going. In 1997, when Bob did his book, *52 More Offbeat Texas Stops*, he put me in it. I'm stop number twenty-nine. Page ninety.

Meanwhile, I was selling my "Drywall Man" cassettes for five bucks apiece. I sold them all over the United States. One guy in Florida ordered one, then he ordered six, then he ordered twelve, then he ordered twenty. A guy in Canada ordered fifty of them. It's just weird. I still get letters from all over the world about that "Drywall Man" song.

I knew I had something going for me, so I started writing more songs so I could make me more cassettes. I wrote what I thought was the world's longest song. It was six or seven minutes long and was called "Heartbeats of Love." I sent it to the Guinness Book of Records. They wrote me back that they didn't know how to judge it, but they passed my name on to a guy named David Isay at National Public Radio. He came down from New York and did a story about me that aired on Morning Edition. That was in '92 or '93.

Right after that aired, I got a call from Chicago, from the United States Gypsum Co., wanting to talk to the Singing Drywall Man. They make drywall, you know. They was real interested in me and still are, so I wrote some songs about United States Gypsum and met some guys from the company at a hotel over in Dallas and played them for them. They really liked them.

I wrote a song about Wolf Brand Chili and recorded a radio commercial for them. Stuff just kept going on like that. Last year, I was on the Terry Dorsey show on KSCS-FM. A guy named Brad Paisley was on the show, too. He had a song called "It Didn't Have to Be" that was the number one song in *Billboard* magazine.

Terry Dorsey thought Brad and I should sing a song together, so we sang "I Saw the Light." I sang the first verse, and he sang the second, and we sang together on the chorus. It made me feel real good, since Brad had the number one song in the nation. I'm hoping maybe he'll help me record some of my songs.

Oh, and I was on the Daily Show on Comedy Central last year. They called me from New York out of the clear blue sky, and they came to Greenville and interviewed me about being the Singing Drywall Man and filmed me, some of it right here in my house, singing "Drywall Man."

Shortly after that, I got a call from Fox television. They said they were thinking about doing a show called Bizarre Behavior, and they wanted me to audition. So I sent an audition tape to them. They sent it back with a just a little note that said, "Thanks, Big Bill."

I perform all over this part of the country. In October I performed several times at the Greenville Cotton Museum during the Greenville Cotton Festival. We had a coffeehouse in Greenville for a while, and I performed there once a month.

I don't want to go too far. I don't want to be another Garth Brooks and travel all over the world. But I don't mind going to Royce City, or maybe as far as Rockwall.

Between the music and the drywall, I've made a good living. I haven't gotten rich, and I know I've got a lot of age on me, but I haven't yet what you call peaked.

Currently, I'm in this movie, *Boys Don't Cry.* I'm an extra in it. I'm walking out the Hunt County Courthouse door and down the steps. *Boys Don't Cry* has been nominated for all kinds of awards, so I'm real proud to be in it.

Somebody from Vamos Productions saw me in that, and they want me to be a sheriff or a Texas Ranger in a movie called *Atanasia*, about Spanish people and stuff that happened to them. It's a speaking part. They're going to film it next spring down at Kingsville. I've written a song for that, too. There's a possibility they'll use it in the movie.

That's what I'm excited about right now.

Alfred Martinez is the oldest surviving member of the family that founded
El Fenix restaurants. He still works in the downtown Dallas restaurant.
Courtesy *The Dallas Morning News*, Jim Mahoney, photographer.

Alfred Martinez

Alfred Martinez, seventy-five, is board chairman of El Fenix, a chain of fifteen Mexican restaurants in the Dallas-Fort Worth area. He also is the host at the downtown Dallas El Fenix. His parents, Miguel and Faustina Martinez, opened their first restaurant in 1918.

My oldest sister, Irene, was born in 1916. My brother Mike was born in 1918, my sister Hortencia in 1920, Henry in 1922. I was born in 1924, Gilbert in 1926. He passed away just seven or eight months ago. Reuben was born in 1930, and then Tina, my youngest sister, in 1935. My father used to say, "One stick you can break over your knee, but eight sticks tied together will be much harder to break."

My father worked hard all his life, even as a kid. He came from the old country, Mexico, around 1910. He was from the state of Nuevo Leon. The little city he was from was close to Monterrey. My mother was from Chihuahua, south of El Paso. They didn't know each other in Mexico. They met here in Dallas, in the part of town they called Little Mexico, about 1915, and that's when they got married.

When he first came over, my father worked laying ties for railroads and streetcars. Then he found out there were so many days it rained and he wouldn't be able to work, and on days he didn't work, he didn't get paid. So he decided to get him an inside job.

He worked at the old Oriental Hotel, which later was the Baker, washing pots or anything that needed doing. It didn't pay as much, but at least he had an income that he could depend on every week.

In 1918, he decided to open up his own little restaurant, at Griffin and McKinney. That's where we started. We lived right across the street. Eight of us children were growing up together, all dedicated to El Fenix. My father, he figured when we got to a certain age—ten-, eleven-, twelve-years-old—we could help in some way or other.

In 1925, he moved the restaurant up the street a couple of blocks, across the street from our present location [1601 McKinney Ave.]. We were there until 1966, when we had to sell that property to the city or the state so they could build the Woodall Rogers Expressway.

There were a few small Mexican restaurants in Dallas back when we started, but not so many like there are today. I don't know of any Mexican restaurant in Dallas today that's older than El Fenix.

El Fenix is a name that's used on a lot of different businesses in Mexico. Hotels, bakeries. That's where my father got it from. It goes back to Greek mythology. El Fenix was a bird that every 400 years, as it gets ready to die, it dives back into the flames, and then it rises again from the ashes, bigger and stronger than before.

My father, he toughed it out through the Depression. I went to Travis Grade School, up here on McKinney, and went on to North Dallas High School and graduated in 1941. Then right after I graduated, war came along. Japan bombed Pearl Harbor. December 7, 1941. The war took most of the young men who were working for my father, and me and my brothers.

I figured if I waited for them to draft me, I would have to take wherever they wanted to put me. So I decided to go and take the cadet test for the Air Force and, lucky enough, I passed it. It was called the Army Air Corps then. I went through the pilot training and got my wings and commission.

They sent us first to Las Vegas, Nevada. We were flying B17s, and that was air gunner school for the kids who wanted to be tail gunners, belly gunners, side gunners and so forth. We were there for a while, then our squadron was sent to Tampa, Florida. The next step would have been to England, but before we could go there, Germany surrendered. And then Japan surrendered, and there wasn't much use for the Air Force overseas. They started discharging right and left.

I came out of the service with a single and multi-engine rating, and I stayed in the reserves for three years after the war. I stayed until the point where I felt like I had to make up my mind: Is it flying, or is it the restaurant business? I decided to stay with the restaurant business.

Before I went to the war, I was going with a girl named Anita Nanez. She waited for me, and a few months after I came home, we got married. In January of '46. We have four children and three grandchildren.

Anita got into politics and eventually got elected to the Dallas City Council. She served two terms. She also started the Ballet Folklorico. She puts more hours into that than I do at my job.

When I got out of the service, there was still only one El Fenix. My father passed over the business to the brothers and sisters, and we started expanding, first to Oak Cliff, then to Lemmon and Inwood and Casa Linda and some of the shopping centers.

Three of my brothers have passed away. There are only two brothers and three sisters still living, out of the eight who grew up together. We and some of the nephews and nieces are still running the business. We have fifteen restaurants now.

Different members of the family have their own departments to take care of. One of my brothers does the book work, and I have nephews and so forth. I myself didn't care for an office job, so I'm out in the field, in service. This restaurant on McKinney Avenue being our biggest, I spend most of my time here.

We serve an awful lot of people for lunch every day, and we have real good dinner business on Fridays and Saturdays. And we have a promotion on Wednesday, the Enchilada Dinner Special, that brings in a lot of people.

El Fenix hasn't been hurt at all by the explosion in the number of Mexican restaurants that's going on around us. We're having our best years ever. There's room for everybody who can make it.

The restaurant business is easy to get into. A lot of them open up, and they're in it for a while, and then they're out again. Sometimes the guy who opens it gets tired of all the work and hires an inexperienced manager to take over for him so he can have more time at home and so forth. Then things start downhill.

That's the first problem against you in the restaurant business: confinement. You have to be there all the time. And a lot of them go out of business because they're underfinanced. They just have enough money to open up, but if things don't develop the way they thought, pretty soon they're out of money.

But anybody who has good food and good service will have a successful restaurant. If you do that, the customers will find you. I like the old-fashioned tacos we have on the menu. A lot of restaurants use those shells now and just stick the taco meat and the salad in it. The old-fashioned tacos are deep-fried. That's much better.

The first El Fenix was a very small place. A counter and maybe a table or two. That's what I heard. It opened in 1918, and I wasn't born until 1924. Then they moved across the street to a bigger place. Then in 1938, my father remodeled and enlarged.

We were the first Mexican restaurant in Dallas to have air-conditioning. That was a big attraction. Back in those days, they used ceiling fans. Now restaurants still use ceiling fans, but they're more for decoration than anything else. The blades are just barely turning.

But good food and good service, that's what it's really all about.

Pat Arnold gets a kiss from one of her dogs, Snuggles, at her home and kennels near Eustace, Texas. Mrs. Arnold and husband take in orphan dogs, but have a hard time getting anyone to adopt them. Courtesy *The Dallas Morning News*, Louis Deluca, photographer.

Pat Arnold

Pat Arnold and her husband, Bill, began rescuing stray dogs in 1993. By 1997, they had twenty-four dogs living with them at their twenty-one-acre compound near Eustace, Texas. Now they have forty-six and have become Straydog Inc., a tax-exempt, nonprofit corporation.

Bill and I made a vow that every dog we take in, they're never, ever going to have to suffer again. If we have to keep them forever, we will. But our goal is to find them homes like Ashley went to.

Many months ago, a neighbor drove up our hill with a little shepherd dog in the back of his truck. He had been working along the roadside with his son, and a truck went past them kind of slow. The truck had a dog in the back. They saw the truck stop, and a man got out and took the dog out of the back. He put her down beside the road and sped off.

He had deliberately come there to dump the dog. The neighbor went down and picked up the poor thing. He knew about us. He asked if we could take her, because he had several dogs and couldn't take another. We were full. But she had nobody. My God. They look at you with that look in their eyes, saying, "Somebody help me." So we took her. We called her Ashley.

Our vet spayed and vaccinated her and checked her for heartworms. While she was at the clinic, we called Cassidy Jones Lumber Co. in Mabank and ordered the chain-link fence sections to make a kennel for her. They sent their truck right out. They always do. They're so kind. We built a shelter for Ashley and got her a doghouse so she would have a home.

Then a wonderful couple called us—Sue and Dwayne Osborne. They were looking for a certain kind of dog, and Ashley fit the description perfectly. This was several months after we had taken her in. She looked marvelous.

I took Ashley to the Osbornes' house, and they fell in love with her. Oh gosh. In two days, it was as if Ashley had been a part of their family forever. They call and write us and have the cutest things to say about Ashley. It's beautiful.

All the dogs deserve this. But I think we've adopted out only ten dogs in the six years we've been taking them in.

When people dump their baskets of puppies and kittens and leave them on the roadside, they probably don't even think of what's going to happen to those animals.

We've found dogs who had parvovirus, gunshot wounds, broken bones, mange, heartworms, hip dysplasia. We've rescued dogs who were locked in yards. Their people just up and moved away and left them to starve or die of thirst. Their family pets!

Skipper is one of our newest ones. He's been with us about a week. A gentleman had seen Skipper wandering around his neighborhood. He knew he was a stray. One day the man saw that Skipper's whole little front leg had been chewed up or mangled. I can't talk about this without getting teary-eyed. And his little back legs were messed up. He had been in a dogfight or something.

The man took him to the Lakeside Animal Clinic in Gun Barrel City, which is where we take our dogs. He wanted Skipper to have medical attention, but he couldn't keep the dog. The dog had nowhere to go. He was on antibiotics for infection, and his little leg was all bandaged up. So I told the clinic we would take him.

We had no place for him, but we couldn't refuse. We've always taken the guys who have no one to help them.

Our other newest one is Snuggles. She's a little white spitz mix who had been a mama dog and a stray. She showed up at a neighbor's, and the neighbor came over to tell us. She looked sick, so I took her to the clinic, and she does have heartworms. She'll be treated for them as soon as she's spayed. We don't want her going into heat again. Everybody here gets spayed or neutered. We always take care of that right away.

Our vet bill is humongous. It hovers around $3,000. It just doesn't go down. Well, it goes down. We make payments on it. Then it goes right back up again. Our vet has been wonderful—Dr. Damon Stephen. He never says anything about how much we owe him.

Teddy Bear and Happy have been with us six years. Little Briar was a wild dog. We rescued her and her brother, Bobby, along with their mama. I noticed Briar was wobbling back and forth. I took her in, and her knee needed major surgery from a birth defect. Her bill was over $400.

Bobby had hip dysplasia pretty bad, so he had an operation for that. We've had a lot of dogs who had to have that operation. We've treated several for parvovirus. We have six being treated for heartworms.

And there was Jack, a beautiful black Lab that one of our contributors found in Dallas. He couldn't keep the dog, and the Humane Society said they were full. So we took in Jack. We kept him for a year, but Jack found a home.

This wonderful couple in Lucas, Texas, called and wanted a dog to be a companion to their dog and their child. Tom and Wanda Grisak and Jason. Jason's a sweet little boy. Bill and I drove all the way to Lucas with Jack. About ninety-seven miles. It took us almost two hours. But we like to check out the homes. We want to make sure they have a fenced yard. We want these dogs to have a wonderful life. Wanda e-mails us all the time, saying, "Oh, Jack did this and Jack did that."

Little baby Annie we found about a month ago. Her mother and four brothers and sisters had been hit by a car and killed. They were a litter, about six weeks old. How Annie survived, we don't know. She was huddled up against the mommy's body. A man picked her up. These are the ones we have, the ones who have nobody.

On December 30, 1997, we got our 501(c)(3) tax-exempt status. Donations for the dogs are deductible now. That took a year of struggle. We had to keep sending the IRS all kinds of information. We didn't think we would live through it.

We were hoping to get big donations from foundations that would keep us going, but that hasn't happened. We still have the same supporters. We have about 250 regular contributors who send us money. One sweet little gentleman in Arizona sends his $3 donation every month. I write him back a cheery little note and send him a picture of the dog he helped save.

These wonderful, wonderful people are like my closest friends, and I've never even met them. If it hadn't been for them, we would never have survived. We've heard from people in Arizona, people in Pennsylvania, in Arkansas. But most of the people who have helped us are from Dallas. Dallas people are wonderful.

I write back to everybody who sends us a donation. But it's a constant struggle, making ends meet, not knowing whether we'll have enough to get through the month.

Randy Harris, our kennel manager, comes to work at four-thirty every morning, and he and I feed the dogs. At seven o'clock, one of our other workers, Ginnie Hodges or Sue Van Ry, starts walking the dogs.

Every single minute, we're doing something for the dogs. They're fed twice a day. We change their drinking water daily. We take two at a time to the big play area and turn them loose and let them have fun.

From one o'clock until six-thiry, I go into each kennel and sit with each set of dogs for a while—there are two in each kennel— and brush the ones that need it and check their ears and try to clip their toenails. Every day. I couldn't bear not to visit them.

They're all happy dogs. We're never going to let them suffer again, ever. Ever.

Bill pays all our living expenses. He works for a printing company in Dallas. There are still times when he has to pay for the dog food, but basically he's no longer the dogs' sole financial support. He and I take nothing of what's contributed for the dogs. That's in a special bank account. We send our financial report to whoever wants it.

Why do people treat these poor dogs the way they do? How can they dump them when such bad things are going to happen to them? I get real emotional when I talk about this. I'm so sorry.

Bell's Barbecue manager Bob Walker at the downtown Dallas establishment before it closed after forty-four years in operation. Courtesy *The Dallas Morning News*, Huy Nguyen, photographer.

Bob Walker

After forty-four-and-one-half years on the job, Bell's Barbecue manager Bob Walker, sixty-three, locked up the downtown Dallas stand and retired.

I've worked forty-four-and-one-half years without missing a day. I've been a blessed man. I've never been sick. In fact, I've never even been to a doctor. I eat barbecue every day. I have a hot link for breakfast and some good old barbecue with some fat and barbecue sauce on it about two o'clock.

I've never taken a vacation. Just the normal holidays and when there's a death in the family. Those are the only reasons I ever close.

I've never failed to make it to work on account of weather, either. Some way or another, I've made my way downtown. It has been slick sometimes, a lot of people slipping and sliding, but I've always made it. I've been open five days a week, seven A.M. to five P.M., for forty-four-and-one-half years.

Back when this old Santa Fe Building across the street had the garment manufacturers in it, we were open until three o'clock on Saturday, too. But when it got to where there wasn't much going on downtown, we started closing on Saturday. From then on it's been just five little old twelve-hour days.

I get here at six so I can open at seven. I close at five so I can leave at six. It takes all morning to open and it takes all evening to close. It takes twelve hours to cook the meat. So I come in and get the fire going, first thing. That's the main thing.

Everything's by the clock. You learn what time certain customers get here, what time the coffee crowd arrives, what time the lunch crowd arrives. Probably seventy-five to eighty percent of my customers are the same people every day. I know what they want before they ever get up to the counter. I've been running the place by myself for the last year. If I run five or ten minutes late, it really puts me in a crimp.

People have asked me, "Are you going to travel when you retire?" And I say, "Yes, I am. I'm going to travel from here to DeSoto, Texas. I'm going home. I've been away from home for forty-four-and-one-half years."

It's been a hoot, I tell you.

Nobody knew it was going to last this long when I started out. March 5, 1955. That was the first day I worked for Mr. J. T. Bell. I worked two hours a day. He and I got along real good together, so I started working a few more hours a day.

Mr. Bell had his first place in 1945 down there on Field Street. Then in 1954 or '55 he moved to Jackson Street. He had a place about half a block up from here, then decided he would open up this second place and put me in charge of it.

People would ask, "Why do you have two places so close together?" We were so close we could throw rocks at each other. But we were both very busy.

Mr. Bell had always wanted this location and, when it became available, he took it. We had the two places for about twenty years. After he closed the other Jackson Street place, Mr. Bell and I worked together here. He's eighty-three now. He's been retired eight or nine years.

I was going to Draughn's Business College when I started working for Mr. Bell. I was working at the First National Bank at night. That's where so many people got their help in those days, from Draughn's Business College and the other business colleges around. You'd work a couple of hours a day, and then you'd go back to your classes at the business college.

I grew up near a little town in Arkansas called Nashville. We lived in this old farmhouse with a fireplace and we had to cut wood every day for our heat and build a fire every morning. When I graduated from high school, I said, "I'm going out to Dallas,

Texas, and seek my fortune. I'm going to Draughn Business College, and I'm going to work inside an office building and I won't have to chop wood and build fires anymore."

My mother, when I wrote and told her that I had quit the bank and gone into the barbecue business, bless her heart, she sat down and cried. She thought she had a banker in the family.

You never know what life holds for you. Who would have ever thought I would be building a fire every morning for the rest of my life? Life takes some funny quirks, doesn't it?

At the time I started working for Mr. Bell, everybody downtown was very busy. I mean, you couldn't walk down the street without holding your elbows in, because there was people running hither and thither. There was no outlying shopping centers. It was all downtown. If you wanted to go shopping, you came to downtown Dallas.

There was a barbecue stand on every corner. I mean literally every corner. And every barbecue stand had all the business they could handle. We all worked together. If we ran out of bread, we would borrow from some other stand, and if they ran out of bread, they would borrow from us.

I married Mr. Bell's daughter, Janice. She worked at the phone company for a while and would come down during her lunch hour and eat barbecue and visit with us. And on her breaks sometimes, she would come down and pitch in and help us. We worked as a family, you know.

I've been with Mr. Bell forty-four-and-one-half years and I've been married to his daughter just forty-two years. I've been with him longer than I've been with her. People say, "So you married into the barbecue business?" and I say, "No, my wife did."

I got in with good people. We've pulled together all these years. Janice has been retired for several years. As our three children grew up, they all served their time down here, too.

People ask me why I don't sell the place, instead of just closing it up. That would be up to Mr. Bell and the landlord. Bell's Barbecue is still in J. T. Bell's name. I'm the manager. That's the way it has worked out for us all through the years, and we like it that way.

There isn't much in here to sell anyway. Everything's pretty much wore out.

And not many people out there want to devote twelve hours a day to a business anymore. My children, my grandkids, they know I never missed a day of work in more than forty-four years, and that doesn't interest them at all.

I'll be forever beholden to Mr. Bell, because I met the love of my life and the livelihood of my life all in the same family. It worked out great. It has been a really nice relationship, both at home and at work.

It's been a hoot, I tell you.

Now I'm sixty-three-and-one-half years old. I want to play golf two or three days a week. My son lives in Houston. We don't get to see him much. My family lives in Arkansas. I'd like to go visit them. I've got a shop I work in there at the house. I like to garden. I've got an acre to take care of. I like to write a poem now and then.

You know, a lot of people think success is getting what you want. My philosophy is, happiness is loving what you get.

I'm used to eating barbecue every day. I'm going to miss it more than my customers will. So I bought me a barbecue pit on the way home the other day. I'll be cooking some brisket.

Billy Roy Switzer entertains audiences as a one-man-band. Courtesy *The Dallas Morning News*, Jim Mahoney, photographer.

Billy Roy Switzer

Billy Roy's One Man Stage Band has performed at the State Fair of Texas almost every year since 1983. The man who plays all those instruments is Billy Roy Switzer. The dog who sits on the stool beside him and examines the crowd is T-Bone. Their phone rings in Denton, Texas, but they live mostly on the road.

My right hand plays a piano and my right foot plays a kick drum. The toes of my left foot play the snare drum. The heel plays the high-hat cymbals. My left hand plays the keyboard bass. And I blow the harmonica. That's six.

The first year I played at the fair, I set a goal to take my six instruments and multiply them by two and somehow play twelve. So I started adding instruments.

Number seven is a cross between a crash helmet and a tambourine on the front. I call it a "helmarine."

Number eight is in two parts. It's a cymbal that sits on a stand and I hit it with a knocker that screws into the back of my crash helmet. I call the cymbal a "ring" and the knocker a "wong," so the instrument is called a "ringwong."

Number nine is a cowbell I play with my left knee.

Number ten is a spur attached to a tennis shoe. I roll the spur down a rub board. I call it a "rub 'n' roll."

Number eleven is a big cymbal I hang from the ceiling upside down and I hit it with the stick on the back of my helmet. I call it a "head banger."

Number twelve is a fiddle. I play it with my left leg. I attach the bow to the high-hat stand and strap the fiddle to my left leg. While I play the high-hat and the snare drum with my left foot, the fiddle moves up and down on the bow.

When I was a kid, before I even started to school, my dad had a country band. Bill Switzer and His Dude Ranch Cowboys. He ran an oil company in Sanger and he was a Denton County commissioner about four times, but he also sang and wrote songs.

Every one or two weeks, the guys in the band would come out to the farm house where we lived and record a fifteen-minute show that was on KDNT in Denton every day right before lunch. Sometimes Dad would have me singing on the radio with his band.

Some of those guys were really good musicians. They didn't read music. They would sit around and put these songs together. "Well," they would say, "what key we going in?" They would work that out and take off.

Sometimes on a Saturday night, Dad and some of the other musicians would go over to Shreveport to the Louisiana Hayride. He was over there the night Elvis made his debut playing there.

After that, my dad would dress me up in a little Elvis-looking suit and paint some sideburns on me and send me down to the Lions Club or anybody who wanted a little entertainment, and I would pantomime "Hound Dog" and do that hoochie-coochie move. I would do it to Elvis' record. I was five or six years old.

When I was in the third or fourth grade, my mother made me start taking piano lessons. She would make me sit and practice thirty minutes a day, Monday through Friday. But I wouldn't be practicing my notes. I would be practicing something I heard at school or on the radio.

I was developing my ear instead of learning to sight-read. I'd get the piano teacher to play through the song she was trying to teach me, and I would start picking it up by ear. She realized I had this talent and was going to do it anyway.

Whenever we had a recital, she would make me play a tune that was strictly by music and then she would let me do one by ear. Of course, the one I did by ear always sounded better. More natural, you know.

I must have taken piano lessons three or four years.

I didn't start being a one-man band until I was twenty-seven. I was running a service station and convenience store out on Interstate 35 in Sanger. I was working about seven days a week, a lot of times eight days a week to keep it all going.

But I had an old upright piano at home in my living room and I would sit down at it and play a few tunes. I wanted some more music to go along with my piano, but I was so busy I didn't have time to catch up with any other musicians. I was living in a small town and there probably weren't any musicians there anyway.

So I remembered I had an old drum set I played when I was in the FFA band in high school, and I dug around in my garage and found the old kick drum. I put it by my piano and started playing it with my right foot. I started playing the high-hat cymbals with my left foot. I was just playing those three, you know, just having fun.

Someone heard it and said, "Hey, that sounds pretty good. You ought to play for dances." So I invented a foot-operated snare drum and started playing keyboard bass with my left hand and started blowing a harmonica.

I started performing professionally about 1977, but I always had another job I worked at. Now being a one-man band is all I do. If I'm not busy doing shows, I'm busy getting ready to do one, or getting something new rigged up. I average about seven shows a day here at the fair. I'll do 150-something by the time the fair is over.

This year I've played a lot of fairs in Oklahoma and Kansas, smaller fairs. But I've played all the way from the New Jersey State Fair to the California State Fair out in Sacramento. And I've played a lot of fairs in between there.

I don't like to call myself a one-man band anymore. I've had to quit doing that because it was confusing to people. In one-man-band terminology now, you say that and somebody will say, "Aw, yeah, we have one of those down at the Ramada Inn." And it'll just be somebody singing along with a drumming machine.

So I say, "Don't call me a one-man band. Call me a *real* one-man band, because I play all the instruments live. Nothing artificial, nothing automatic." And there's only one other guy I've seen do that. I heard of another guy up in Denver that does it and I'd like to meet him sometime.

There's also an older guy that came up to me last year in Kentucky. He was in his 70s or 80s. He had been doing it forever, but he owned a sausage plant. He never did it that much professionally. Just for fun, mainly.

I didn't get to see him play. He showed me a picture. He played a guitar, blew a harmonica. He had made a snare drum out of a washboard and a bass drum out of a big wash tub. I'd like to have heard him play. Maybe I can sometime. His son was a state representative or something in Kentucky.

Here at the fair, I play the songs the audience wants to hear. It's a hard crowd to play for. I mean, they're out here to have fun, but there's so much to do at the fair, and things are moving on pretty fast. Unless they really like what you're doing, people won't stop, because they've got Johnny pulling on them, saying, "Let's go to the Ferris wheel!" and Sally pulling on them, saying, "Let's go see the animals!"

But when I get ready to play all twelve instruments, they all stop to see what that's going to be. And those that stay, they'll pat their foot.

I play songs that I think will keep their interest. If I play too many slow songs, they'll say, "Aw, naw, naw," and go sit down or something. So I try to keep it upbeat.

At a fair, if you're not up on a sixty-foot tower and setting yourself on fire and diving into a gasoline pond, people are not going to stand there and watch you very long. That's about what it takes to keep somebody's attention at a big fair like this. You've got to be pretty interesting.

I've been on the road about forty-eight weeks out of the last year. Some of the shows are short festivals, weekend things. Of course, I like the longer fairs like this, where I can sit in one place and make more music, instead of setting up and tearing down and moving so much.

The more I play a song, the more I can do with it. I can add more licks. After all, I'm supposed to be a musician. And for me to play all those instruments, every inch of my body has to know every song.

Paul Hastings, a three-job man, works as a greeter at CompUSA, Sam's Club, and Lowe's, all in Addison. Unlike his competitors, he greets customers with song. Courtesy *The Dallas Morning News*, Randy Eli Grothe, photographer.

Paul Hastings

Paul Hastings, sixty-two, is a cheerful man. He greets customers at three different businesses in Addison and far north Dallas, and has developed a distinctive way of doing his job. The lines here that are in italics were sung by him during the interview.

I work at CompUSA at 3800 Belt Line Road, and at Sam's Club at 4150 Belt Line Road, and I've just landed another job at Lowe's Home Improvement Warehouse on Inwood. I work those jobs during the day from six in the morning till nine-something at night.

I try to get up at five o'clock in the morning, but I can never make it on time. I usually get up at 5:02. I prepare myself for the day, eat an egg and a half, two pieces of bread, mayonnaise and chocolate milk for breakfast.

I get in my Lincoln Town Car and drive up to Lowe's. I work there from six o'clock until nine in the morning. Then I go over to Sam's. I start greeting people, helping them upgrade their memberships, getting them to sign up for the Elite program and switch their membership to a credit membership.

I work at Sam's until three o'clock. I have to be at CompUSA at three-thirty. Sometimes I eat a snack in between, sometimes I don't. I'm at CompUSA until nine-something.

I also manage a disabled Vietnam veteran twenty-four hours a day, part of the time by cell phone, part of the time at his home every day. I manage his whole life. His social life, his financial life, his home, his animals. I take care of him.

After I finish at CompUSA, I traipse down to the house where I live on Wycliffe. The veteran lives in the front of the house, I live in the back. When I walk in the door, the veteran and his dog can jump into bed and go to sleep. He likes somebody there when he's sleeping.

I go to my apartment in the back and go to sleep until 5:02. So technically I'm working twenty-four hours a day. I don't call it work, though. I think it's a lot of fun.

At my jobs, I say, "Hello, how you doing?" At Sam's, I say, "May I help you in any way in Sam's Club? Have a good day." At CompUSA, I say, "Are you on a journey that you can complete without help, or do you need somebody to help you?" If they need somebody, I go find the right person.

Then I say, "Have a good day. It's be-good-to-yourself day at CompUSA. So go buy something for yourself." I do little things like that all day long.

The thing I do different is I sing these things. I've been singing little ditties every time I open my mouth for a long time. For many years, every job I've had has been along Belt Line Road. Fresh Choice gave me a gig for a while when they opened up. Then I went to Spaghetti Warehouse when they were there. They didn't leave because of me, but they did leave. Now Humperdinck's is at that location. I also worked at Gill's Crab Shack. Years ago. All of this has been along Belt Line Road.

During the past seven years, the only thing I've done off Belt Line Road is this new job at Lowe's, where I work on my off time and show people where every one of those two billion screws in that place is.

Before I got into these greeting jobs, I was into property make-readies as a contractor, the MPH Corp. A make-ready is when somebody moves into an apartment and they live there from a week to five or ten years and they destroy the inside of it. When they moved out, my company would go in and make the place ready for the next person. Painting, cleaning the carpet, exterminating, changing out the drapes, repairing holes in the walls. And it would become a beautiful home again.

I did that a lot for four or five different real estate companies. I had a lot of people working for me for ten or twelve years. I did a lot of other things during that period, too. I've always been a workaholic.

But it never seems like work to me. It's fun. I have a wonderful time going to work.

My first work experience at Sam's was right before Christmas seven years ago. People were running in at the last moment to buy everything, and they would drag their kids in there after they had been shopping at the malls all day long, and the kids were crying and whining.

So I would try to change their focus. I started singing things like: *Oh, you better watch out, you better not pout, 'cause Santa's coming on his way.* Stuff like that. That lasted through Christmas, then I quit singing.

But people would come up to me and say: "Can you sing to us now?" Or: "Where's the song?" It just caught on. Everybody wanted to hear me sing. I don't know why. They started calling me "Singing Sam." "Sing it again, Sam," is what they would say. My name isn't Sam, but I was working at Sam's, so I guess that's why.

I have this wonderful feeling that Sam Walton [the founder of Wal-Mart and Sam's Club] was enjoying that, because that's what he liked to do. He liked to make people happy, and that was my major goal. I knew Sam Walton. Not real well, but I knew him. I visited with him a few times and I've read about him. And I try to keep Sam's spirit alive, no matter where I am. He's my mentor, I suppose. I like to make people happy. The happier other people are, the happier I am.

I started at CompUSA almost two years ago. They came down and asked me to work for them. They said, "We want you to do for us what you do for Sam's." They wanted me to sing.

There have been a few people who don't like what I do. I've had people complain about me. It's usually people who don't like anything. One guy wrote a letter to the home office of Sam's in

Bentonville, Arkansas. He sent it to the president and all the vice presidents of Sam's and Wal-Mart. He said he was just going to quit shopping at Sam's because of what I do.

I had to read that letter about two weeks later, and I was really feeling down while I was reading it, until the manager said, "Read the back side." And on the back, a vice president had written, "Paul, keep up the good work. One in thousands is not bad."

I don't know why some people don't like my singing. I think some people don't want recognition of any sort. They don't want anybody to say hello to them. They probably consider it an invasion of their privacy. Although they're in a public store, they think no one should talk to them. But if you don't talk to them, you're not waiting on them like you should.

One time a customer complained, and I was told not to sing anymore. I didn't sing for two days. The third day, the manager called me into his office and said, "You can sing whatever you want to whomever you want. If they don't like it, they can shop somewhere else." In those two days, they had had like 200 letters complaining that they weren't letting me sing.

At Sam's, people hear me all over the store. One lady wrote that people don't have as bad a time standing in long checkout lines if I'm singing.

I have close to 500 little jingles that I do. Like: *If you want to have a good day, come on down to Comp-USA today.*

And: *Did you think about having a real good time, so you wound up down at Sam's on Belt Line Road in the little bitty town of Addison, Texas, where the sun nearly always shines real bright except at night and on rainy days and cloudy days and foggy days and the days it snows real hard on Belt Line Road.*

I try to make the kids happy, because the parents love their kids, and if you make over their kids, the parents will be happy, too. I thank the kids for bringing their parents to the store. *I'm glad you drug your mother and your daddy in with you.* It tickles them.

I'm having the best time of my life. I don't think there's any-body who's happier than I am. I love what I do. I love to hear people say, "Thank you, Paul."

Ouida Johnson retired after forty-two years at The Children's Center of First Community Church. Mrs. Johnson began as a teacher and later ran the program as the school's director. Courtesy *The Dallas Morning News*, Karen Stallwood, photographer.

Quida Johnson

*Since 1971, Quida Johnson, seventy-four, has been
director of the Children's Center, a school associated
with First Community Church, 6355 E. Mockingbird Lane in Dallas. She's retired now.*

I'm from Malakoff, Texas, population around 1,200. My dad was
a physician there for years. Malakoff was a coal-mining town. It
mined lignite coal for Texas Power & Light. Of course, when the
electric company went over to gas, that closed Malakoff down.

I came from a schoolteacher family. Back in those days, about
all a woman could do was teach school or be a nurse. When I went
away to college, my mother insisted that I get a teacher's certificate. For security. For insurance. But I never intended to use it. I
was a secretary for an oil company for many years.

Then when my daughter Janice was old enough to come to the
Children's Center, I enrolled her, and there was an opening on the
staff. They hired me. I've been here forty-two years. I taught four-
year-olds for fourteen years, then in '71 I became director.

This place has been the joy of my life. Every day, I've looked
forward to coming to work, because we've had such wonderful
children and supportive parents. If every school could have what
we have here, we wouldn't have the problems today that the world
is experiencing.

I've had a tenured, dedicated staff of fourteen people who kind
of got handpicked through the years. All of them except two had
children who came to our school. One teacher I had a few years
ago had been here eleven years as a parent, and I felt that what I
saw in her parenting skills was really more important than certification.

That's kind of true with all of them. They don't all have teacher certification, but they have what I think is really necessary for working with little children: patience, energy, and liking children. Those are the basics.

The children are two-and-one-half years old through kindergarten. Three years after I became director, I decided we had to get a movement program started—a physical movement program—for the children because of television. Television has been the worst thing that's ever happened to little children. It hurts their motor skill development.

So we put in a movement program in 1974. The bonus we got out of the program was that it also worked on the children's listening skills. Television also has a bad effect on their listening. They tune out the world and don't hear what you say to them.

I watch children's cartoons myself sometimes, just to see what they're seeing on television. They kind of make me jumpy. The approach to children's programming is really very bad. There's even violence in children's cartoons. If I were four, sitting there watching that stuff, instead of seventy-four, I think I would be out of control.

I've said many times that if we could get rid of television for a few years, it would cure our problems. Kids today just sit there staring at it. They're missing a sense of wonder. They aren't exploring God's world.

I'm a firm believer that children learn what they live. I can see it in them as they walk in the door. It's so obvious what goes on at home. It's in their attitudes. We have very few rules here, but one of them is that we will never take the respect away from a child, but we will also never allow a child to take our respect from us.

Nor our dignity. And we don't take the dignity from a little child. Each child is a child of God and unique. We want to keep them unique. We're not trying to put them all into a mold.

My whole goal has been to create a happy, loving atmosphere for the children, where they could experience God's world, learn to make decisions, and be motivated to the joy of learning.

Tone of voice is the secret to teaching little children. You don't raise your voice to a child. And if you don't, they don't. They're getting your role-modeling. I think if you're too harsh with a child, you take his dignity from him. They're just learning. They don't know everything that's right and wrong.

Of course, you never hit a child or spank a child. The only way of handling a child's discipline is with a timeout. And a very short timeout at that. Because at this age, all you need to do is distract them. And you tell them this is not acceptable behavior here, and we don't do that.

We hear a lot of talk about family values these days because of what's happening to our young people. Yesterday at six o'clock in the evening, I took my grandsons up to Blockbuster to get a movie. I was appalled at what I saw.

It seemed the whole world was rushing in, barefooted, with no shirts, to get a movie for the evening. I'm sure they then stopped and got pizza to eat while they were watching the movie. This is where family communication is breaking down. They're not talking to each other. They're sitting and watching videos and movies.

It has been very harmful to our young people. Families should be talking to each other and doing things together. Not on the computer all the time. I have respect for the computer. We have a computer lab here. But there isn't a balance. Communications are breaking down among families.

Old as I am, I grew up without television and video games. We played in the sand and the water. Of course, the world was different. You could go outside and stay all day long and play without your parents worrying about you. I think little children today are really handicapped because they can no longer go outside and play without their parents' worrying that they're going to be kidnapped.

The children leave our school at twelve o'clock, and they have to go to gymnastics and ballet and all kinds of things. It's all structured time. They don't have time to be a little child.

Children play what they live. They mimic their parents. You can almost hear the parents talking through the little children. You get a feeling of the respect that everyone in that family is shown, or maybe disrespect. You can tell whether the parents communicate with them. You can tell how harmonious their home life is.

I think the first seven years of life is when you really set your character and your pattern of life. It's that early beginning that sets the foundation. I don't think you can undo that.

Parents ought to let little children be little children. Talk to them. Spend time with them. Help them explore God's world.

Bob Colombe cuts the hair of customer Abbey Zimmerman at Preston Forest Barber Stylist Shop. Courtesy *The Dallas Morning News*, Randy Eli Grothe, photographer.

Bob Colombe

*For twenty-six years, Bob Colombe has owned and
operated Preston Forest Barber Stylist at Forest Lane
and Preston Road in North Dallas. Many of the
shop's customers are businessmen, including H.
Ross Perot, whose hair Mr. Colombe has cut every
week for twenty-five years.*

I am of the Sicangu Lakota tribe. Our last chief was Spotted
Tail. Red Cloud was the head of our people back in the days of
Sitting Bull and the others. He was a famous man.

I was born on the Rosebud Reservation in South Dakota in 1939.
I was born at the agency hospital there. It was probably the only
hospital. It was run by the Indian Health Service. My father was a
rancher on the reservation.

In 1958, I guess it was, Congress came up with a plan to urban-
ize the Indians, because the Indians have always been a problem.
Nobody knew what to do with us. Because we were here.

So Congress came up with this program for Indians to go to
school or go to work in the cities. It was a trial deal. The government wanted volunteers. I was eighteen years old. I elected to go
to school. I lived on a ranch. Life wasn't that bad. But, you know,
at that age a kid wants some adventure.

The Bureau of Indian Affairs had field offices all over the country. Dallas was one. San Diego, Denver, Cleveland, Fargo. There
were a number of them. For me, it was a pretty easy choice to
come to Dallas.

The deal was, they would pay you to go to school, then help
you find a job. I think I was one of the first guys that went into the
program.

We were told to go in to the agency office and pick out a vocation. I chose barbering. The only reason I chose barbering was because of the length of time you went to school to learn it. Six months. That was just right. I would go down to Dallas in the fall, go to school during the winter, and in the spring I would come back to the reservation. I never intended to be a barber full time.

A brother of mine, Charlie, came with me. We went straight to school as soon as we got here. There was also a guy from Arizona, a Navajo guy. There was another guy, an Apache. We went to the same school at the same time. American Barber College. It was down on Commerce. 606 Commerce.

What made it real handy was that just up the street, I think it was 912 Commerce, was the field office for the Bureau of Indian Affairs. So we could walk up there and pick up our check once a week. I think it was $30 a week. And that would pay all our maintenance and food and room and everything.

We did OK on that. My brother and I had a room at a boarding-house down on Washington and Bryan. Some other Indian guys were there, too. Probably six or eight Indian guys. To tell you the truth, it was pretty cheap. It was a tough neighborhood. A lot of guys there were on the city dole. Winos, you know.

That wasn't a place we would have chosen to be. We lived there to make the budget work. You could stay there for $12.50 a week, and they gave you one meal, and then you had to have your clothes cleaned and stuff. We didn't have any cars. We rode the bus around. Of course, we didn't go very far. Just up and down from the boarding house to town and back. It wasn't bad.

The barber college was great. We were disciplined. We knew to be there on time and study and practice the practical part of it. We were good students, because we thought that's what was expected of us.

After we got out of school, Charlie went to cowboying and then went into the Army, and eventually wound up back on a ranch in South Dakota. I decided to stay in Dallas. It's a nice city. I liked the city girls. That's about all there was to it.

We got out of school one day and I pretty much went to work the next day in a shop in East Dallas. I worked there a couple of months. Then it was summertime, so I went back home to work on the ranch and ride in some rodeos. I went back and forth for several years. I would stay here in the wintertime and go back to Rosebud in the summertime.

Then in 1962, I met my wife, Marilyn, here in Dallas. She's from Lufkin, over in East Texas. We pretty much settled down. We've got two grown kids, Sheila and Chris. They both live here in town, within five minutes of us. And we've got three grandchildren. I'm well established here.

In '63, I got this barbershop. Forest Lane was way out on the edge of Dallas then. Preston Road was just a little two-lane. The same guy who owned the shopping center then still owns it now.

I run a traditional barbershop. We do a lot of styling, but most of our clients are businessmen who want a regular haircut. Men come in and take a look and say, "Hey, boy, I've found a real barbershop!" They send other guys in.

I still go back to Rosebud three or four times a year. I have five brothers, and they're all there. I have ranch land and farm land on the reservation. But I've always maintained this business, always lived down here in Dallas.

That relocation program didn't work for most people. I think it had a lot of merit. It offered an opportunity for people to do things. But it wasn't well thought out. Moving people all the way from South Dakota down here to get a job, you know. That wasn't for everybody. They were breaking up families. I don't know what their intent was. I think it was to offer opportunities, but they didn't really follow up.

When I checked in to the field office in Dallas, they were very nice, but they sent us to live in the West Dallas housing projects. To me, that was no place for Charlie and me. I mean, we weren't poor. We had a family and a home. We didn't belong there with all those real poor people. It was the wrong thing to do. What I did was just thank them for the ride, and then I went and found my own place.

They didn't understand that. They probably thought I was some dumb guy that they were going to help, but that wasn't really helping me. Nearly everybody who came here in that program went back where they came from. They didn't stay in the city. They missed their families. They didn't like being isolated from the Indian community.

The Bureau of Indian Affairs didn't do their homework. That's pretty much the history of the Bureau of Indian Affairs.

Rabbi Frank Joseph, right, teaching Melvin Korelitz the Talmud in the Irving Havurah. Courtesy *The Dallas Morning News*, Milton Hinnant, photographer.

Frank Joseph

Frank Joseph, forty-two, grew up in Dallas and is the rabbi of Irving Havurah, a small congregation. He's probably the only rabbi in Texas who used to be a country-Western disc jockey.

My mother, my aunt, and my grandmother would go to the State Fair every single year. Some years they would go four, five, six, seven times. They would take me along.

Hank Thompson and his Brazos Valley Boys used to play the fair every year in those days. He would put on about three shows a day. And my mother and my aunt and my grandmother were avid Hank Thompson fans, so I heard him three times a day, every time we went to the fair. I was only a baby, maybe one or two, when they had me on their shoulders, listening to Hank Thompson. It was the first country music I ever heard.

I was too young to really appreciate the greatness of Hank Thompson. He was a huge star back in the '50s and '60s, and now he's in the Country Music Hall of Fame. But being around his music at that young age must have made some kind of impression on me. I've always loved country music.

I love songs that tell a story. When I was five or six, I would get those books by John A. Lomax or Alan Lomax, full of cowboy songs that had twenty, thirty, sometimes maybe forty verses, and every one of them told a story. I loved those cowboy songs. I tried to learn as many of them as I could, because I loved the stories that they told. Around the age ten, I started writing ballads about cowboys, with twelve or fifteen verses.

We didn't have a TV until I was at least eleven or twelve. When we finally got one, I watched all the country music programs that were on late Saturday night. I loved them. I've always loved story songs.

In the early '90s, I was a disc jockey on KNON radio [89.3 FM], which is a public-service radio station in Dallas. My brother Harvey and I had a program called Meridian to Bakersfield. It showcased country music from its earliest days with Jimmie Rodgers of Meridian, Mississippi, to the Buck Owens and Merle Haggard sounds of Bakersfield, California.

Our program covered all of country music, every genre, every style, every type. The station manager had given my brother the name "Lefty" because he's left-handed and because Lefty Frizzell was an outstanding country musician and we played a lot of his music. Since Harvey became known as "Lefty" on the radio, I became "Righty."

Sometimes Lefty and I did the program together, sometimes we did it separately. We were always there at the station together, though. My sister would take the requests. She would answer the telephone and help us find records. So it was a family event for about four years, from 1990 until 1994. Since KNON is a community radio station, we didn't get paid anything for it, but it was a lot of fun.

It didn't matter to us how obscure a song was. If they would just name the entertainer and the song for us, we would have it for them. That was our mission: to bring you whatever country song you want to hear, whether it was bluegrass, Western swing, country rock, Texas folk. It didn't matter. We would bring it to you.

The Top 40 stations can't do that. If a song isn't one that the station deems to be among the Top 40 of the moment, they can't play it. But we could play any song.

Now there were some times we just absolutely couldn't find a song somebody requested. But ninety-nine percent of the time, we came through. And we enjoyed that.

One of the things I like about country music is its social conscience. A lot of people think country music is just about drinking and cheating and honky-tonking. But a lot of country music is about trying to better the plight of man. Man's struggle.

Hank Williams, for example, sang "Your Cheating Heart" and "Your Cold, Cold Heart," but he also sang songs like "Be Careful of Stones That You Throw." All the country musicians do this. They're far, far, far, far deeper than the average person thinks.

This may sound strange, but to me country music is very compatible with a lot of what Judaism teaches. I'm strongly attracted to the part of Judaism that asks, "How can we make the world a better place?" You know, we need to be aware of the plight of other people. We need to put ourselves in their place.

To a large extent, country music does the exact same thing. Hank Williams did it. Even Hank Thompson, the king of Western swing, sang songs like "The Pathway of My Life," which tells a story of forsaken people and misfortunes that happen to people whose sons are going to war.

Whatever social ills we have in our society, country music addresses them, and it always has. Like Reba McEntire's song "She Thinks His Name Was John," about the AIDS problem. Or "A Street Man Named Desire" by Pirates of the Mississippi, which addresses homelessness.

Merle Haggard has a lot of songs that really make a stink about the plight of people. "Branded Man" is about the difficulties of coming out of prison and making a new start. "Irma Jackson" is about bigotry and interracial marriage. And he wrote and sang that in 1970.

When I had my radio show, those were the songs that I would personally spotlight when I wasn't playing requests.

I became a rabbi in 1992 and became the rabbi of this congregation in the same year. I got into the program about the same time I became a rabbi. For a while, I flew back and forth from St. Louis Rabbinical School to Dallas to do the program.

In this congregation, doing the show wasn't a problem. If I had a large congregation, they probably wouldn't have appreciated my taking every Tuesday evening off to be at the radio station. Plus, putting the show together took a long time, looking for the requests. Every Tuesday from five to ten o'clock was radio station time.

I love to play the guitar, not to perform but to relax. To me, the guitar is the ultimate relaxer. What yoga does for some people, the guitar does for me. I play country music and Jewish music for twenty minutes, and I feel like a new man. I did another program on KNON on Sunday nights called the Jewish Music Hour. I wasn't Righty on that. I was Rabbi Frank Joseph. I did that two or three years.

Country music isn't generally popular among Jewish people. But in this congregation, there are a number of people who listen to it. I would say fifty percent of my congregation listens to country music. Or I should say, in about half of our families, there's at least one person who listens to country music. I make tapes for people in the congregation. We swap records and CDs. Prior to 1990, I had almost no Jewish friends who listened to country music.

Country music has become more commercial than it was in the old days. In a way, that's good because it has made country music more popular. On the other hand, country music has suffered for it. Its essence isn't as honest as it used to be. It doesn't come out of real life as much as it used to.

I think Clint Black and Garth Brooks and Faith Hill are very good. They're wonderful musicians. But they're not coming from a personal point of view with that great honesty from the heart like Hank Williams and Merle Haggard did. Those guys were writing about their personal experiences.

There are a lot of lines in country music that are so real and say so much that I find myself quoting them in my sermons to emphasize points. Garth Brooks, Merle Haggard, Hank Williams, George Hamilton IV, I've quoted them all.

Father Efren Ortega, pastor of St. James Catholic Church in Oak Cliff, one of the oldest Catholic congregations in Dallas. Father Ortega is from Colombia. Courtesy *The Dallas Morning News*, Andy Scott, photographer.

Efren Ortega

The Reverend Efren Ortega, sixty-four, was celebrating his tenth anniversary as pastor of St. James Catholic Church in Oak Cliff, the poorest parish in the Diocese of Dallas.

I was born in Samaniego in the south of Colombia. It was a small town, now it's a big town. Now it's full of plantations of cocaine and poppies. Also there are many guerrillas in the mountains around it. Guerrillas against the government. It's a very nice town. I was born February 2, 1935. I'm getting older. But I'm still young in the spirit.

I was an orphan. I lost my father when I was five years old and my mother when I was seven. My grandmother grew me up. The mother of my mother. She was a nice, grand, wonderful lady. I have one sister, older than me. My uncles acted as our parents. They were very nice people.

My sister and I went to the grammar school at Samaniego. I was a good student, and they sent me to another town to the high school, because in my hometown there was no high school then. When I was fifteen I became a Marist brother. The Marist brothers are good educators, a French community. They dedicate themselves to teach in the high schools.

I was a good student, so they sent me to Europe, to Spain, and France. I was there a year, and then returned to Colombia. I was happy teaching the young people in the Catholic schools there in Colombia. But then I became a priest.

How did I become a priest? Brothers are not priests. They teach only. I tell you how I became a priest. I was in Lourdes, France, on a pilgrimage. I was wearing a cassock, as all brothers do. A German soldier came up to me and told me in French, "Will you hear my confession?" I said, "I'm not a priest. I'm a brother." And he told me, "Oh. Just a brother?" He tells me, "Just a brother?" After that I thought, "Maybe I'll become a priest, because I am just a brother."

I was thirty-eight years old when I was ordained as a priest. My dream was working with the poor in Latin America, in the rural areas. Because I was an orphan, you know.

I was ordained in my hometown, Samaniego. The bishop was there, many friends, many Marist brothers, many alumni. It was a happy celebration, a beautiful feast. Very nice. The town band was there, playing music.

The mayor of the town was there, and he asked the bishop why I couldn't just stay there in my hometown. And the bishop granted the request of the people to let me serve there. He appointed me as a vicar—an assistant pastor—in Samaniego. Jesus said nobody is a prophet in his hometown, but I was.

They now had high schools in Samaniego. I was a chaplain and taught philosophy in a school run by the Franciscan sisters, and also at a school named for Simon Bolivar. I had a good reputation. I was there for five years.

Always my dream was to study in another country, to learn another culture, learn another language. Special to me was the United States. People who come to the United States have ambition. It is the best country in the world. All the boxes of things in the stores, everything is made in the United States, nothing in Latin America. Even a box of matches says, "Made in the USA"

I spoke to a priest who had studied at Fordham University in New York and had returned to Colombia. He knew a Cuban priest who had a parish in New York. He said I could get a job in a parish in New York and have plenty of time to study at a university.

My bishop gave me permission to study in the United States. I got in touch with the Cuban priest in New York, and he accepted me as his assistant. I arrived from Colombia in 1977.

The parish was in the South Bronx. The South Bronx is a bad area. They mugged me one day when I went off the subway. Two teenagers. They put a gun to my neck and took $50 from my pocket. I didn't have good English. I said in Spanish, "Respect me because I'm a padre." They didn't understand me. They said, "Stay still." I was so scared.

Then they sent me to a parish in Manhattan. Blessed Sacrament. Very nice. I learned English and passed the test for foreign students. I attended Fordham University at first, but I applied for a scholarship there and they denied it. I applied at another Catholic school, St. John's University, well known for basketball, and they gave me a half-scholarship missionary grant. I studied and worked in the parish at the same time, and in 1985 I graduated with a master's degree in education, in counseling.

I came to Dallas, Texas, because when you have an education you have many options everywhere, especially in America. Even in the priesthood. I came first to the federal prison at Texarkana as a chaplain. I had to have one month's training like everybody who worked there. Doctors, chaplains, everybody. Even firearms training. I failed that. I was very alone there. I lived in a mobile home close to the prison, and I felt very isolated.

Texarkana then was in the Diocese of Dallas. I talked to Bishop Thomas Tschoepe here, and he asked me not to go back to New York but to stay in Dallas because they needed a Spanish-speaking priest at St. Edward's, a parish in a Spanish area. The pastor there was Father Becker, an Anglo, a wonderful man of God. He has died. I was assigned to him for one year.

Bishop Tschoepe retired and Bishop Charles Grahmann took over, and I applied for incardination. "Incardination" means you're no longer strange. You belong to the place where you are. It's like a transfer from the Diocese of New York to the Diocese of Dallas.

I had a bachelor's degree in philosophy from Colombia and a master's degree from St. John's, but I wanted also to have a bachelor's degree in America. I went to the University of Dallas, and in 1989 I graduated in psychology there. I'm happy because I have two degrees from America now. I did it backwards. I got the master's degree first and the bachelor's degree second.

The bishop called me and said, "I have a job for you." He named me pastor of St. James in 1989. Since then I'm still here. I'm happy. I've been working hard. This is the poorest parish in the Diocese of Dallas. We dream of building a new church, but we never reach the goal because the collection here is only $3,000, sometimes $4,000, every Sunday.

It is a neighborhood filled with violence and poverty. There are many drugs, many gangs, many pregnant teenagers, many dropouts from school. I sense their hopelessness. Members of the gangs come to the church as *damas* and *chambelanes* for the *quinceaneras*. One time in a sermon during a *quinceanera* ceremony, I asked them, "Give me the names of the gangs." They raised their hands and told me the names of the gangs they belong to. East Dallas Locos. Bloods. DOC, which means Doing On Crime. Crips. They gave me ten names of gangs around Oak Cliff. Former altar boys are in the gangs. That is the reality here.

You have to have great strength and great love in your heart to work with the poor. We're trying to transform this environment through the suffering Jesus, and also to give an education to our poor people. We have 2,500 families. Ninety percent of them are Spanish, six percent blacks, and Anglo four percent.

In the ten years I have been here, more poor, Spanish-speaking people have moved in. At least twice a month I go to bless the house of Mexicans. They buy old houses cheap and they fix it. That means we're going to have more stability in the neighborhood. We have many young people. More than forty-five percent in this parish are under thirty-five years old. And a lot of children.

My message to the young people is to take the opportunities in this great country. We are in a unique country. Stay in the school. Be proud of your family, of your background. Don't hide your identity. Stay in the school.

Every Sunday, the church is packed. I say Mass four times. I have to put all the children in the sanctuary, around the altar, to give more room for the adults. It's full of children around me while I'm saying Mass. It's beautiful.

Our goal is to carry out the instructions of Christ: "To bring glad tidings to the poor, to proclaim liberty to captives and recovery of sight to the blind, to let the oppressed go free." We must spread his word and help others.

We need a new church desperately. A new church will cost $1.4 million. The diocese is going to give us permission to start building when we reach $500,000. We have been raising money for twelve years. When I came here ten years ago, we had only $12,000. We have so far $325,000. Everything depends on the generosity of the people. But poor people are poor people. They can't give what they don't have. That makes it very slow.

But I am very optimistic. Everything is possible when you have faith. Faith in Jesus, faith in the poor. God works in mysterious ways. I am very sure that we are going to start our new church at the end of this year. I am positive. God calls our church, as a community of faith and hope, to be a source of light in this poor place.

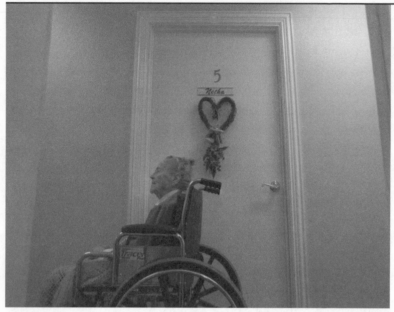

Netha Stanton was a stage, screen, and television actress for many years and still makes television commercials. Courtesy *The Dallas Morning News*, Helen Jau, photographer.

Netha Stanton

*Actress Netha Stanton began performing before
audiences more than ninety years ago. Among many
roles, she played Clyde Barrow's mother in the 1967
movie* Bonnie and Clyde. *She lives in Garland.*

On the Fourth of July I'll be ninety-eight years old. I was born
in Grand Rapids, Michigan, in 1902. That was a long ways ago.
Joan Crawford was my first cousin. Her mother and my father
were brother and sister. Joan's family lived in San Antonio, but
our families got together every few years.

Joan was never nice to me. I don't know why. She pulled my
hair and chased me. We were never close. The last time I was in
Hollywood I decided to call her. I said, "This is a voice from your
dim, distant past. You may not remember me." And she said,
"Well?" She had a sharp edge to her voice. And I said, "I'm Netha."
And she said, "Oh! Well, I'm very busy!" And she hung up.

Joan's real name was Lucille LeSueur. It's a French name. She
never used that name.

I became an actress, too.

When I was a little girl of about three, my mother had a three-
way mirror. It was called a dressmaker's mirror. She gave me her
worn-out window curtains or petticoats or whatever, and I would
dress up in them and stand in front of that three-way mirror, and
I would tell those little girls in the mirror what to do.

I would tell the girl on the left to do something, and she would
do it. I would tell the girl on the right to do something, and she
would do it. I was the director. And they took direction very well.
I was very serious about that. To me, the little girls in the mirror
seemed like people.

The first time I was before the public using my voice, I was a little girl standing by a grand piano. And this little girl was saying:

"My papa held me up to the moo-cow-moo, so close I could almost touch. I wasn't a fraidy-cat. Well, not much. The moo-cow-moo's got a tail like a rope. It's raveled out where it grows. The moo-cow-moo's got soap all over its nose, and the moo-cow-moo has a bag or something. I don't know just what it's called, but it has handles on it. Four of them, and you hold them like this, and you squeeze and you squeeze to get the milk to come out. And I wanted my daddy to show me how he could do it. He would sit down on a three-legged stool and put the pail between his knees, and he would squeeze and squeeze and squeeze. So I tried to do the same. By Jeb, did I squeeze and squeeze, but nothing came out but just a little squirt of milk on my skirt."

I was about three or four. It was at a meeting of the Eastern Star. My mother had been named whatever the high mugwump is, and she was supposed to have some sort of entertainment. So I was her entertainment.

After that I learned little verses, little elocution things, and I gave various kinds of recitations. I was always in demand be-cause—well, I'll pat myself on the back—I had long dark curls and a nice smile and I liked people. I liked what I heard and saw when I was in front of an audience.

When I was in high school, a professional theatrical team came to Grand Rapids to produce its plays at the Powers Theater. At the time, I was acting in a play called *A Prince There Was* on the high school stage. After my performance, a bouquet of flowers was pre-sented to me. A woman from the professional company met me backstage. She had sent the flowers to me. She said, "I'm playing the same part you just played, and I wish I could do it as well as you do." That was a big day for me.

While I was still in high school, I taught elocution and voice. My voice is gone now. I can still talk, thank goodness, but I no longer have the quality or the volume or the control that I once had. We lose a lot of things as we advance in years.

Unlike Joan, I always used my own name on the stage. I was Netha Abbott at that time. I didn't see any reason not to use my own name because I was proud of my name.

I had two Broadway shows. One was *Desire Under the Elms* by Eugene O'Neill. The other play was *A Bag of Dreams*. I don't remember who wrote that. It was a flop. It played only one night. I didn't like the boy who played opposite me. He was very snippy to me. He was a good-looking lad, and he knew it. I've never liked people who put on airs.

When I was twenty-one, my agent called me to Hollywood, and I went there. I didn't crack it. I didn't have what it took. I don't even know what it took. If I had known what they were looking for, I think I could have projected it. But if you don't know what you're supposed to do, how can you do it?

So I went home to Grand Rapids. Later, I would play in many movies, but they were all small parts. Well, there are no small parts, are there? If you take out the small parts, there's no play. So I gloried in the fact that I had a lot of small parts.

I met my husband, Bayne, at a Sunday-school party in Grand Rapids. He was the son of my pastor. Bayne's father was a Methodist minister. I was a senior in high school at the time, and Bayne was a senior at Albion College. We got married about three years later.

Bayne worked for Western Electric in Chicago. In 1954, he got a job as a parts procurement man for Chance-Vought, an aircraft company that had a big plant in Dallas. That's how I wound up here.

We lived in a lot of places in between and had a lot of jobs. Every place we lived, I found out as fast as I could whether there was a group doing plays or entertainment in the town. I always found it. If I didn't find it, I created it. These were all amateur groups.

Most of the films I did were made here around Dallas. The first was *Hell on Horseback*. It was a Western. I played the president of the Ladies Aid Society, who was offended by the language she heard around her. That was in 1954 or '55. I was in *A Bullet for Pretty Boy*, and I was Clyde's mother in *Bonnie and Clyde*.

I was in thirty or forty movies. Most of them are second-grade movies. But *Bonnie and Clyde* is a famous movie. And I was in *Born on the Fourth of July*. That's a famous movie, too. I played a little old lady standing on a curb, and a couple of young kids come through with a big dog. I say:

"Who do you think you are, trying to push me around! This is my birthday, and I came down to see this parade! And I'm going to see it! You get out of here, you little skunks! Get gone!"

Big deal. But, as I say, there are no small parts.

I haven't retired. Kim Dawson is my agent. I've done two jobs in the last two months. One was a TV commercial for a company that makes special foods for diabetics and the like. The other was a radio commercial for wheelchairs and other physical aids.

My husband had big, bushy eyebrows, and one day Kim Dawson said, "I can use those eyebrows." She got him several acting jobs. He played a lead in a film for the Baptists called *Insurance?* and I was the director.

We had three daughters and adopted a son. I only have one daughter left. She's now seventy-five. She lives in Miami. My husband passed away four years ago. He had Alzheimer's. I took care of him for five years. Alzheimer's is a terrible thing. He was such a brilliant man. He was a whizbang.

I've had a beautiful life. A wonderful life.

Eighty-three-year-old Fred Bruner is one of the patriarchs of the criminal law profession in Dallas. Courtesy *The Dallas Morning News*, Ariane Kadoch, photographer.

Fred Bruner

Fred Bruner practiced criminal law in Dallas for many years and was known for the incredibly long string of acquittals he won before Dallas County juries. He participated in the Roe vs. Wade case. He and his wife, Joy, live in Highland Park, Texas.

I was born in Quanah, Texas, eighty-three years ago. I went to the Oklahoma Military Academy in Claremore for my last two years of high school. It was a school for the cavalry. Will Rogers and Wiley Post used to come by there all the time before they were killed in a plane crash up in Alaska. After that, I went to Baylor University in Waco, and after that I went into the Army.

I enlisted in 1942, right after Pearl Harbor. I only had one eye, and I was 4-F, but I wanted to get in. So I waived my eye and went as a buck private to Camp Robinson at Little Rock, Arkansas. From there they shipped me to an MP outfit in New York Harbor.

A captain up there called me into his office one day and said, "Why don't you go to OCS?" And I said, "Well, I'd like to go to cavalry OCS, but I can't because I've got only one eye. And he said, "I can get you into the Signal Corps at Fort Monmouth, New Jersey." So I said, "OK."

After I was a Signal Corps second lieutenant, they shipped me down to Tampa, Florida, where they were putting together a company to go to Hawaii. They didn't have enough people to make up the company, so they told me to go down to the guardhouse and get sixty men who were there on minor offenses and fill up the company with them. Which I did.

I put them on the troop train with me, and we were going through Mississippi. Every time the train would stop, I'd put an MP up front and one in the back and two on each side. And these old Red Cross ladies would come out, and they would say, "Is this a prisoner-of-war train?" And I would say, "No, ma'am. These are GIs. They're going overseas." And they would say, "Do you have to take them over under guard?" And I would say, "You do these guys."

We got over to Hawaii and put these radio stations up on top of a mountain there on Kauai. Those sixty fellows from the guardhouse turned out to be the best men I had.

I stayed through the war on Kauai and the big island of Hawaii and came back and went to law school at SMU on the GI Bill. In 1948 I went to work for the Dallas County district attorney's office under a man named Will Wilson. He later went to the Texas Supreme Court. An old lawyer down at the courthouse said, "The reason they want Will Wilson on the Supreme Court is they want the layman's point of view." Anyway, I worked for Will for two years. Then when Henry Wade ran in 1950, I quit my job and went out and campaigned with him. Later I worked for him.

In the meantime, I was dating this girl who was a former Navy nurse in San Diego. She lived here in Dallas at the time. About the time we got married, the Korean War broke out and they called her back into the service and sent her to Corpus Christi. They were about to put her on a hospital ship called *Repose* to go to Korea.

I went to see Henry Wade about it. He said, "Well, why don't you go over and see Mama in Rockwall. She knows Sam Rayburn real well." Rayburn was speaker of the House at the time. So Henry Wade's mama called him on one of those old crank phones and told him Joy had already served in World War II and the whole story, after they talked about the cotton and the corn and everything.

Mr. Rayburn said, "Let me look into it." The next day I got a telegram from him saying orders were being issued for the immediate transfer of Lieutenant J. G. Joy Bruner to the naval air station in Dallas. I took the telegram down to Corpus Christi and showed it to her.

Joy was at the Dallas Naval Air Station when our first child was born, who's now forty-nine. She's a lawyer in San Antonio.

We had six children in all. Two of them and a daughter-in-law are lawyers. We have eleven grandchildren.

We had a lot of times together, old Henry Wade and I, years ago. Anyway, I left the district attorney's office in 1957 and went out in private practice with a lawyer named Sam Daughtery. We handled every kind of case in the world. I don't mind saying, at one time I had won more murder cases than anybody had ever won here.

My most famous case of all was *Roe vs. Wade*. I was representing a doctor in Carrollton who was charged with abortion. Of course, we went to the Supreme Court in Washington. A girl named Sarah Weddington from Austin was the lawyer who was really instrumental in the case. She asked me to come into it before it went to trial.

Another case I handled, a guy named Patel was charged with murder. He was from India. In India, the name "Patel" is like "Smith" in the United States. He was an engineer, but he killed his wife. He said he killed her because she was having an affair with a ballplayer here in Dallas. That was before we were in the big leagues. It was the Texas League then.

After he killed her, he put her in the trunk of his car and took her to his office and put her in the icebox there. One day an employee walked by and opened up the icebox and out came the body. That was how they found out Patel had killed her. Of course, our defense was that she was having an affair. He said the reason he put her in the icebox was because he intended to cremate her later.

Well, the jury went out and found him guilty and gave him ten years. He went to Huntsville. I went down to see him two or three times.

I got to tell you one more story. While I was prosecuting, they had a big campaign on for DWI cases. The Traffic Commission they had at that time sponsored all those cases at the courthouse. Joe B. Brown was the trial judge, and we were trying this case in front of a jury. There was a lawyer in town (I'm not going to call his name; he's deceased now), he was supposed to be real mean, and he called me a liar in front of this jury.

And I said, "Don't you call me a liar again." He called me a liar again, and I hit him and knocked him over the railing back where the spectators were sitting. Old Joe B. Brown jumped up off the bench and said: "I find you in contempt of court! I give you three days in jail and a $250 fine!"

So a bailiff named Barksdale carried me over to the jail. Bill Decker was the sheriff. He had already heard about this through the reporters who were covering the courthouse. Decker said, "Fred, do you know where the back door is?" And I said, "Sure do, Sheriff."

So I went out the back door. Next day, a fellow from the Traffic Commission gave me an envelope with $500 in it. So I made some money on the deal. I was thinking maybe I ought to hit people more often.

I got to tell you one more story. I knew Jack Ruby real well. As you know, he killed Lee Harvey Oswald. Very shortly after my wife and I saw Ruby kill Oswald on TV, Jack Ruby's sister, named Eva Grant, called me. She said Jack wanted me to represent him. I told her I would go down to the jail and talk to him the next morning.

In the meantime, that night, the TV put on Jack Ruby's entire history, going back to Chicago, where he was connected to the rackets. So the next morning I was going down to the jail at City Hall, and I kept thinking about the things I had seen on TV. I thought, "I'd be a fool to get in that case." So I sent a note up to Ruby that I wasn't going to represent him. Which I didn't.

I practiced law in Dallas almost fifty years, until about four years ago. I learned that you win or lose a case when you pick the jury. You've got to know something about human beings. I used to tell my juries: "Stand up in that box and tell the district attorney you're not going to tolerate his bringing accusations against citizens like this."

If you've got any kind of a defense at all in a case, you ought to be able to win it.

Ellis County Judge Al Cornelius, near an abandoned Superconducting Super Collider building near Waxahachie. Courtesy *The Dallas Morning News*, Irwin Thompson, photographer.

Al Cornelius

Al Cornelius, sixty, moved to Waxahachie in 1991 to work on the Superconducting Super Collider. When the federal government killed the project, Mr. Cornelius stayed and got elected Ellis County judge.

From 1967 through mid-'91, I worked in contracts and procurements for NASA in Houston. Every time they would do a space flight, they would take some of the administrative people and let us work in Mission Control, to get us familiar with what was going on in the technical side of the house.

I happened to be assigned to Mission Control during the Apollo 13 flight. I was managing the telemetry machine, keeping track of how the astronauts were doing medically. It was a pretty simple job.

Well, as you know, Apollo 13 developed a problem. And everybody who was working in Mission Control during that crisis got the Presidential Medal of Freedom.

So I got one. I'm one of the very few administrative people to ever get that medal. It's on my wall at home. I like to point it out to people and say, "There's my medal. Where's yours?"

I was still working with NASA when I got a call from a friend who was with the Department of Energy, and he told me about this program called the Superconducting Super Collider. He wanted to know if I was interested in coming up here and working on that.

At the time, I was chief of procurement operations at NASA, and I was contemplating a move out to California to work on the space shuttle program. But I came up here to Waxahachie to talk with them about the Super Collider project, and it didn't take me long to realize this was really where I wanted to be, rather than in California.

I'm a native Texan. Not that I wouldn't fit in in California, but I just like Texas better. And the Super Collider program was an opportunity to do something unique. So in August of '91 I moved up to Waxahachie.

The Super Collider program folded in the fall of '93. I wasn't surprised. It was a political thing. There were senators and representatives in Congress who were just determined that, because it wasn't in their state, they were going to kill the project.

Also, the Department of Energy has to bear some of the responsibility for not adequately explaining and publicizing what it was we were doing. There were a lot of physicists working on the program. When I asked them how we could better explain to the public what we were doing, it was very difficult to get a good answer.

We should have been able to say in layman's language that it wasn't just going to be a big tunnel to see how many quarks we could find, or how many parts to the atom. There were practical applications to be made. But people around the country thought it was just another government boondoggle.

It disappointed me that the Super Collider was killed, but it didn't shock me. So I asked for and got early retirement from the government.

Even when I was working at NASA, I had been contemplating getting early retirement somehow. I wanted to get into public service, but as a federal civil servant, I couldn't be involved in any kind of political activities.

I started thinking about what offices I would like to run for someday. I volunteered in law enforcement. I was in the Harris County Sheriff's Department as a reserve and ultimately wound up working as a homicide detective there. So when I retired from the federal government I thought maybe I would run for constable. Then I was persuaded to run for justice of the peace instead.

But the longer I talked to folks, the more it became apparent that they wanted me to run for county judge. I had to give that a lot of thought. Being county judge is a pretty hefty responsibility.

I finally decided this was a job where I could use the skills I had developed in management, because so much of the job of county judge is administration.

So the day I retired from the federal government, in December of '93, I came down here to the courthouse and signed up to run.

There was some concern that because I had lived in the county only a short time—not quite two-and-one-half years—it may work against me. Some of my political opponents still call me a carpetbagger. They're still trying to tell people that I moved here from up north to take over this county.

It's funny. We get a good laugh out of it. Actually, I was born in Goose Creek, Texas, went to Robert E. Lee High School and wore a Confederate uniform in the school band. "Are You From Dixie?" was our big song.

The only time I ever lived in the North was at the very end of my tour of duty in the Navy. I trained recruits in Illinois for a while.

It turned out all right. The people here were very receptive to the plans I talked about for the county. They don't care whether you were born in Waxahachie or in Goose Creek. They want somebody who will do a good job of managing the affairs of their county.

One thing that helped me get to know the people and for them to get to know me was that for about two years after I moved here, I wrote a weekly column that ran in about seven newspapers in the county. I was the crime prevention officer for the sheriff's department, and I wrote about family and social issues.

People got to know what kind of person I am and what my values are through the writing I did. People I had never met would come up to me on the street. They knew I wasn't some foreigner moving in here.

So everything worked out just real fine. I'm in my second term now.

We're getting things done. We have one of the lowest tax rates in Texas. For the first time in history, we're restoring our court-house. The Ellis County courthouse is the second-most-photo-graphed building in Texas, after the Alamo. We're building a new administration building down the street. We've got the county's first transportation plan in the works.

When the Super Collider was killed, people were predicting that this county would die on the vine. But we managed to stay on our feet, and now we're one of the fastest-growing areas in all of the state. For the first time, people in the metroplex are looking south.

Up until now, it has been Plano and Denton and up in that area. But this area is so attractive now because of the inexpensive land. Industry is moving here. Good, clean industry. People are moving in here to live.

We've done all right. We're in good shape.

Artist and Elaine Thornton are founders of the Artist and Elaine Thornton Foundation for the Arts, which introduces minority children to the arts. *The Dallas Morning News*, Kim Ritzenthaler, photographer.

Artist Thornton

*Artist Thornton, fifty-four, and his wife, Elaine,
own Metro Media Buyers, a Dallas advertising
and public relations firm. They also founded and
head the Artist and Elaine Thornton Foundation
for the Arts, which promotes artistic activity
among minority youth.*

Anna Black, my grandmother, was an artist. She played the blues. She knew Blind Lemon Jefferson personally. She drank a quart of beer a day and started playing the blues at ten o'clock in the morning. Piano and guitar. She played until at least ten o'clock at night. She died when she was ninety-eight.

She named me. All the other children in my family had normal names—Larry, Eddie, Sally, Thomas. But Anna Black saw something, knew something, felt something. I guess she marked me to be an artist. Ever since I was a little fellow, I could draw. I drew on paper sacks from the supermarket. Clowns, dogs, birds, horses.

I grew up in Sticktown. That's what everybody called our section of the north side of Fort Worth. It was kind of like Watts in Los Angeles. The Santa Fe Railroad ran along the east side of it. The south side was bordered by the Trinity River with its terrible smell. On the east side were also the Swift and Armour and Rosenthal packing companies.

We used to walk through the stockyards down to North Main to the Isis Theater. We called it the Isaac Theater, but it was the Isis. I guess it must have been eight miles to go to the movies.

On the 19th of June—Juneteenth—they would clean out some of the stalls in the stockyards and put down hay and bring in big old barbecued halves of cows and big tubs full of soda pop. There would be just a big old thing down there in the stockyards. My daddy was a butcher for the Rosenthal Packing Co., and the company would do that for their employees. So did Swift and Armour.

Sticktown was the lowest echelon on the ladder. In that part of Fort Worth, you had Greenway, which was kind of an upper-crust kind of society; then you had Hamilton Park, which was middle-class; and Sticktown, which was the bottom. Nobody in Sticktown looked down his nose because everybody was looking up, trying to figure how the hell to get out of there.

I went to Ninth Ward Elementary School. James Cash went to Ninth Ward, too. He was the first black basketball player at TCU. He's a professor at the business school at Harvard now.

Sticktown was a rough situation. I went to school up to the seventh grade. My father died when I was nine, and Mom had eight kids. She worked as a maid in the Fort Worth Hotel downtown. She worked at Colonial Country Club, making salads. She cleaned house, she scrubbed floors, cooked, she made hats and stuff. She made do.

I was the next-to-oldest child, so I figured if I could get out of there it would be easier for her to feed the others. Maybe I could send something back, too.

I tried to join the Navy when I was sixteen, but I didn't test out good, and they wouldn't take me. I studied a whole year with correspondence courses and what have you. I passed the test, and the Navy sent me to Great Lakes, Illinois.

Later, I was on the USS Waddell, which was stationed at Long Beach, California. We were the "innocent ship" that LBJ said the North Vietnamese fired on in the Tonkin Gulf. They fired on us, all right. We were trying to pick up a pilot who had been shot down off the coast of North Vietnam. I was part of the boat crew that pulled the guy out of the water.

I got my GED while I was in the Navy and enrolled at Long Beach Community College when I got out. I went to a couple of other community colleges, and to Pepperdine for a year. That was before it moved to Malibu, when it was still in the 'hood. Then I went to Columbia and got my degree in communications.

When I got back to Texas, I went to Baylor for a year and SMU for a year. When they told me I would have to go still another year to get a master's, I said, "To heck with it. My GI Bill is almost up." I still wound up owing SMU a little money.

I was trying to do something that had never been done in my family before. My mama had gone through the fifth grade, and my dad had gone through the third grade. I was trying to do something to help out. Not just my family, but maybe to send a message to young people that, hey, you can do something. Not to say that everything is all rosy and pretty, but to say that, although times are rough, if you have determination, there's a way. Just because you start out slow doesn't mean you're going to finish last. And not everything is the world's fault.

That's why I'm so proud of our son, Artist Jr. He has built on what I did and gone beyond me. He's got his bachelor's and master's in English and communications and is working on his doctorate over at TCU now.

A lot of youths today think, "To hell with that. I want it all right now." When I was young, I had the same attitude. People were saying, "Hey, man, Martin is all right, but Malcolm is saying, 'Let's stop singing and start swinging.'" Young people tend to go in that more emotional, let's-get-it-on kind of way.

I met Elaine at Studio Watts in Los Angeles. I had just gotten back from Vietnam and out of the Navy and was trying to figure out what the heck was going on. I had been over in Vietnam, fighting for democracy, and I come back and Watts is burning. Bill Cosby started Studio Watts right after the Watts riots, and he was teaching improvisation there. We were studying acting under Larry Hagman.

Elaine and I started the Artist and Elaine Thornton Foundation for the Arts about ten years ago. We had an advisory council over at the South Dallas Cultural Center when we first opened it up, and the foundation grew out of that. We didn't want to be restricted to working just with the Cultural Center, but with other arts organizations as well.

It has been going pretty good. It's up and down, as far as getting support for it is concerned.

The function of the foundation is to use art as a tool for positive social change. Not to do dramas just for the sake of doing dramas, but to do dramas that say something. We're not trying to whip anybody over the head, but we want to make people think.

When we did Charles Fuller's play *Zoo Man and the Sign*, for example, we wanted people to look at and contemplate the consequences of gang violence on the individual and the community.

It's our responsibility as adults to point the way for our children, to give encouragement. Not necessarily to say, "This is right and this is wrong," but to say, "Now this is what's happening. You make the judgment."

And if they're off, then you pull them back and say, "Hey, that's not the best way to deal with that. You're not looking at it clearly."

We're trying to open up children and break down barriers between grown-ups and children.

Everybody has his own way of getting there, wherever that is. And if we understand who we are and where we come from, then we can understand where the heck we're going.

Art is one way of doing that. It worked for me. I've drawn and painted all my life. I do a little acting. I try to help the kids know the joy of these things.

I guess my grandmother knew I would do that. So she gave me my name.